Women in Revolutionary Egypt

T0352104

Women in Revolutionary Egypt

Gender and the New Geographics of Identity

Shereen Abouelnaga

The American University in Cairo Press
Cairo New York

This paperback edition published in 2019 by
The American University in Cairo Press
113 Sharia Kasr el Aini, Cairo, Egypt
200 Park Ave., Suite 1700, New York, NY 10166
www.aucpress.com

First published in hardback in 2016

Dar el Kutub No. 26164/18
ISBN 978 977 416 928 1

Dar el Kutub Cataloging-in-Publication Data

Abouelnaga, Shereen
        Women in Revolutionary Egypt: Gender and the New Geographics of Identity / Shereen Abouelnaga.—Cairo: The American University in Cairo Press, 2019.
        p.   cm.
        ISBN: 978 977 416 928 1
        1- Feminism—Egypt
        2- Women—Political activity—Egypt
        305.42

1 2 3 4 5   23 22 21 20 19

Designed by Sally Boylan
Printed in the United States of America

If I didn't define myself for myself, I would be crunched into other people's fantasies and eaten alive.

—Audre Lorde, *Sister Outsider*

CONTENTS

Preface ix

Introduction: Whose Spring? 1

1. Is There Gender in This Revolution? 13

The Road to 2011 13

State Feminism: What Is It Good For? 16

The Marriage of Nationalism and Gender 19

Women's Agency 24

The New Geographics of Identity 26

Beyond Gender 31

2. Gender and the New Text 35

New Generation and New World 36

The New Transversal Text 39

The Visual 42

The Eye of the Beholder 48

The Iconic 53

The New National 55

3. The New Subversive Poetic Voices 59

Sara Allam: Kisses and Loneliness 63

Marwa Abu Daif: Mother and Military 68

Sabrin Mahran: Breaking the Law   73
Sara Abdeen: On the Edge   78
"Without Huge Losses"   81

4. Multiple Patriarchies and One Body   **85**
A Utopian and Modern Moment   87
Fragile Bodies   91
It Is All about the Body   93
Islamic Bodies   95
Why Do They Hate Us?   98

5. The Politics of Memory   **107**
The Rise of Memory   108
Trauma of the 25 January Revolution   114
Documentations of Memory in Social Media   116
Gendered Memory after the Eighteen Days   117
Shattering the Silence of the Body   124
Historical Memory   128
Then What?   131

Notes   **133**
Index   **147**

PREFACE

The increase in the tendency to read the position of Egyptian women in isolation from as big an event as the Revolution was reason enough to make me write this book. On one side, the Western media—in all its forms—worked on highlighting the violations of women's rights and bodies; on the other side, it totally ignored the wider sociopolitical context that is replete with protesting voices and sharp consciousness. This vision led to the portrayal of Egyptian women as victims and implied a naïve attitude toward women. Similar to the Revolution, which has been challenged by its countermovement, the narrative of women was sidelined by its own counter that appeals more to minds that still believe the white man's burden exists. The way women have been exercising and performing their agency is unprecedented. This has not gone unnoticed by scholars of the region, and Egyptian academia is to be credited for having realized that at a very early stage. As the new geographics of identity has prevailed to enrich gender with other elements, the academic scene has kept up with developments. This book, however, does not assign itself the role of reading what happened since the eruption of mass protests in 2011; understanding the past opens potential possibilities of new forms of agency in the future. It is important, then, to fathom the meaning of agency this book employs.

I am indebted to the feminist minds that have challenged the social and political norms, and I have questioned the canonical theoretical principles. I am also indebted to all the feminist activists and scholars I have known and who never hesitated to transfer their experience. However, my main inspiration has been Susan Stanford Friedman's book, *Mappings*. Friedman's project of going beyond gender has informed my book and allowed several exits from theoretical impasses. It has also helped me understand situations that seemed totally incomprehensible, because they did not correspond to the expected or what 'should be.' The high fluidity of the political scene has called for a constant change of subject positioning, a fact that had been totally foggy and nebulous for me and others as well. Any change of positioning seemed to call for vilification and condemnation. Amid the disappointments of the revolutionary trajectory, Friedman's theory worked like a deus ex machina. Identity is ipso facto flexible, fluid, and changeable, but amalgamating feminism, multiculturalism, poststructuralism, postcolonialism, literary studies, and cultural studies for the purpose of reading the new geographics was the real inspiration. My thanks are also due to the American University in Cairo Press, especially Neil Hewison, whose trust enabled me to start the project, and Nadia Naqib, whose patience and support helped me finish. I must also express my deep gratitude to my editor and first reader, Caitlin Hawkins.

INTRODUCTION: WHOSE SPRING?

And when we speak we are afraid
Our words will not be heard
Nor welcomed
But when we are silent
We are still afraid

So it is better to speak
Remembering
We were never meant to survive
From *A Litany for Survival* by Audre Lorde

Water, water, every where,
And all the boards did shrink;
Water, water, every where,
Nor any drop to drink.
From *The Rime of the Ancient Mariner* by S.T. Coleridge

"Gender, gender everywhere, and not a space to win." Starting from March 2011, I kept almost humming this line in parody of Coleridge's famous line in his Romantic nineteenth-century poem *The Rime of the Ancient Mariner*. Unconsciously, I started humming it after the shameful virginity tests perpetrated by the military, but wasn't that too early? Perhaps, and perhaps not. I view this incident as a warning sign that worse incidents were bound to follow. The arguments and logicalities that ensued were disappointing and shocking, and they meant that the gender battle had erupted. The analysis of that incident was confined to whether it happened or not, emphasizing how authority (the military at that time) tends to oppress women. In the case of Samira Ibrahim, a victim of the virginity tests, nobody ever raised the issue of her origin (Upper Egypt), her age, her class, and her veil. These were essential factors that should have been taken into consideration to understand how gender—as a main component—will seek real agency. They were factors that, in the past, should have worked against the victim; paradoxically and fortunately, they worked for her. Without the Revolution, nobody could have sued the authorities. One wonders how between January and March 2011 society was capable of breaking the fear barriers.

The transformation of the sociopolitical scene was a corollary of the Revolution. It was neither positive nor negative transformation; just transformation—a substantial change and a conspicuous shift toward the readiness to confront. The scene was overpopulated with voices and actors whose main concern was to designate and fix what came to be called 'Egyptian identity.' The appearance of the identity discourse signified a crisis that was political, intellectual, ideological, and societal. In addition to going back to the obsolete definition of identity as fixed, stable, and unchangeable, gender was taken to be a marker of identity. This explains why the former Mubarak regime was so concerned with controlling and legitimizing a certain system of gender—one that consolidates the power of the patriarch, in his multifarious manifestations, especially the father figure. Consequently, women's agency was hindered, and women were forced politically and discursively to conform to a monolithic 'modern' image that has shielded all the sociopolitical and cultural differences and problems.

How the 25 January Revolution endowed women with the opportunity to initiate the route to agency while struggling over identity construction is the main concern of this book. I want to examine the emergence of women's agency in the post–25 January moment, and, in order to do that, we have to trace many ideas back in time. The history of certain ideas could, in turn, trigger the history of gender. For example, the history and trajectory of nationalism in Egypt since the beginning of the twentieth century is, in my view, the history of the women's movement. Authoritarian regimes always find an excuse by which to control the people's choices, to limit their practice of agency, to shrink their space of appearance, and to channel their anger through false causes. Women, on the other side, usually pay double the price as subjects and as women. The power of the central state and its system has always been so tight that the Revolution never managed to demolish them. Yet, every power carries within it the regimen of resistance. If the Revolution demolished anything, it was the principle of homogeneity; it turned out to be a mere illusory notion, propagated for a long time by the state. The Revolution has allowed for the eruption of differences previously silenced and suppressed through the incessant celebration of homogeneity through the state-run media. The Revolution marked the appearance of a real diversity on several levels: ideological, cultural, religious, educational, class-based, and gender-oriented. The revolutionary act has functioned as a political and cultural shock that effected subversions in a previously solid national gendered discourse. Nonetheless, the refrain remains, "gender, gender everywhere, and not a space to win."

The mise-en-scène of Tahrir Square revealed the fact that there are several constructs of gender; simultaneously, rethinking gender was a necessity. In this sense, the Revolution acts as an eye-opener to the gender issue. A new era that requires a new approach. However, it turned out that it will be much more complicated than one can imagine, especially with the rise of multiple political factions. Amid this mishmash of power relations, the poignant link between gender and nationalism comes to the fore. The first consequence of the rise of nationalism is always the trivialization of women's rights. There are always more pressing and urgent issues that the nation needs to address. Due to this high-pitched tone of nationalism (that comes close to chauvinism), the space for lobbying for and supporting women's rights has become frayed and thin. Certainly, the link between nationalism and feminism in the Third World is as old as Kumari Jayawardena's book,[1] maybe older, yet what is reemerging is not the nationalism of postcolonial periods. What we have now is nationalism in a new cloak: it is the nationalism of the patriarch.

With all the long-deferred aspirations after performing agency, women were quite aware, more often than not, of the risks that lurk in adopting a feminist discourse that mistakes the discursive formations of gender identity for mere sexual difference and for an additive element of nationalism. Direct and unmediated, women's presence in the Egyptian Revolution was so inspiring that it could not pass unnoticed; many analysts have conflated such "space of appearance"[2] with the public sphere, which in itself was conflated with nationalism and with the streets. Unfortunately, at the toxic crossroads of culture, religion, and politics, women lost their "space of appearance," and the female body was turned into a site of different ideologies. This is where the confrontation and the process of identity construction started, on one side, and co-option and usurpation, on the other, became irreversible. The female body has become a text that must be read against the grain. That is to say, it is a text about how women turned physical violations into a tool of rewriting the culture of the body and is essential in understanding the new gender positions. One cannot say that the task is already complete. What matters is the discursive dynamics that managed to change the stagnant position of gender that was limited to sexual differences.

The most important aspect, however, of gender transformation in post-Revolution Egypt is that of positioning. Starting from March 2011, it was obvious that power circulated in a very complicated way, and this allowed the subject to reenvision and rethink the issue of positionality that was previously governed by class. The network of power that lacked transparency allowed the subject to adopt multiple and contradictory positions, hitherto unthought of. The Revolution functioned as a traumatic eye-opener where alliances were revised and where the possibility of connection across other factors, in addition to gender, was very liable to happen. The new situation generated a new text. The manifestations of multiple gender subject positions through new forms of expression constitute the new text of the Revolution. Perhaps the term 'text' has undergone a radical change in Egypt recently (the Revolution itself is a text). The rise of a new revolutionary generation meant, among other things, the rise of new texts fully independent of the state's authority and, thus, completely oppositional. The female body, in this sense, is an oppositional text, if not one of revolt. Bringing these texts into focus, and, consequently, constructing a new narrative that relocates gender in the Revolution is the aim of this book.

Interestingly enough, when women felt that the Revolution had demised, they came up with other ideas that would sustain their presence in the public sphere. They resorted to ordinary activities and the practices of everyday life. Having taken to the streets for a long time, women developed new strategies of resistance that I perceive to be a "collective action by non-collective actors," as Asef Bayat presaged early in 2010.[3] The trajectory of this resistance meant that women were (and still are) caught in the highly contesting controversy of identity politics where a new lens of analysis other than patriarchy or misogyny should be adopted to read the complex picture. In general, it is in the daily micropolitics that women were capable of asserting their vision by bringing the personal and aesthetic into the political and public. The politics of memory and what the women's culture of protest chooses to forget and to remember was (and perhaps still is) another means of resistance to the attempts at homogenizing and subduing gender.

Several convincing arguments have focused on the alleged rise of democracy and the concomitant fall of women's rights, a situation that has been termed the "gender paradox"[4] and "democratic paradox."[5] The combination of rising political camps that attempted to co-opt gender as a means of establishing a foothold resulted in the formation of the new geographics of gender identity; these have been drawn discursively, aesthetically, and visually in spite of the "gendered grammar of violence"[6] and in the face of all the gendered politics of an imagined nation.

Many readings of the Revolution were baffled about the position of gender and, indeed, if there was any gender in the Revolution. Mostly, they reached the hasty conclusion that women's rights were in crisis. It is true that women activists had to face several ambivalent moments where triumph and danger were intertwined. The successive political shifts in Egypt, the rise of religious fundamentalism, the increased militarization (and masculinization) of the country, and the naturalization of neoliberal values along with global hegemonic privatization pose new challenges to the concept of gender and its role in identity formation. The problem lies in the way the elements of the revolutionary scene were dismembered. Islamists, women, the youth, workers, for instance, were each dealt with separately. This arbitrary separation contradicts and negates the spirit of the eighteen days (25 January to 11 February), that is, the point of departure. And, thus, the point of arrival was erroneous. Women were everywhere and so they should not have been viewed as standing as a category on their own. This meant that the voices of the rising generation could not be taken to be a manifestation of a shift in the strategies and vision of women. This generation uses a different discourse and lexicon; its alliances are completely transversal, and, most importantly, its strategies of resistance transgress the expected and traditional.

Chapter one explores the road to the Revolution and the entanglement of gender and nationalism. The Revolution created a context where the encompassing rubrics 'women of the Third World' or 'Muslim women,' for instance, do not mirror the novel circumstances Egyptian women have to confront and engage with. Neither do these rubrics explain the complex interplay of powers where women's agency and position are constantly negotiated. The new cartography of struggle has to be read in a context that takes into consideration the micropolitics of everyday life as well as the larger processes that work on separating the private from the public and political. The scene needs to be looked at afresh to understand how the new rising generation is resisting discursively and strategically the fixation of identity, simultaneously relocating it in a geopolitical, wider context. In addition, the new transversal alliances and coalitions have set free the potential fluidity and flexibility of identity; thus, allowing women to exercise agency in a highly turbulent and politically polarized location that works against them. Thus, rethinking gender in the light of the new revolutionary discourse is a means of rewriting culture or, rather, reading it against the grain. Audre Lorde had every right to say that "the master's tools will never dismantle the master's house";[7] it takes completely novel strategies and means to do so.

The new revolutionary generation has managed to negotiate new tactics of identity politics by going beyond gender, without abandoning gender. That is why the Egyptian political and cultural context requires a new approach to analyze women's discourses of positionalities that led to the discursive formation of agency. Susan Stanford Friedman's "locational feminism"[8] is the most valid lens through which women's position can be understood. Gender, one constituent of identity, is not adequate to fathom the strategies and discursive formations undertaken by the new rising revolutionary generation to counter the current web of regressive power relations. The main goal is to find out how the discourses of positionalities set free the analysis of gender from the Western feminist methodologies. At the same time, one cannot overlook the fact that there is a strong revival of a nationalist–feminist discourse that prioritizes nationalist issues and, thus, deprives gender issues of their due centrality. Since going beyond gender means bringing in new factors of analysis, without abandoning gender, then disentangling nationalism from feminism is necessary, unless we want to reproduce the Algerian Revolution discourse on gender that comes close to Hamlet's yell to Ophelia, "Get thee to a nunnery."

Chapter two rereads the nexus of culture and women. Culture is taken to mean the new aesthetic forms, the new text, which established a transversal relation with politics. The Revolution has gained substantial flesh through the artistic expression that reached the point of functioning as a tool of protest and resistance. Taking into consideration the discourse of going beyond gender, it becomes a bit difficult, and also contradictory, to speak about the gendered performance of art. Yet, it is an unforgettable fact that women and art were the two phenomena that directed the attention of the world toward the Egyptian revolution. Can we talk about the role of women and art in the Revolution? They were not assigned a role; they were committed to a revolutionary act. It was a revolution, an event in the world of which women and art formed a big part.

This chapter explores how women managed to assert multiple subject positions not only through art but also through a new established relationship between art and politics. Exploring the concatenation of art and politics in the post-Revolution era will always remain an unfinished task if the past is not also taken into consideration. To understand the relation between art, politics, and gender, we have to go back to the scene before the Revolution where the deep state supported a homogenous artistic scene that guaranteed, unfortunately, a perfect alienation of the arts. Against this backdrop, one can understand how women aesthetically practice what Bayat calls, "The power of presence"; it is a power that exhibits itself as a "collective action by non-collective actors."[9] Hence, the new strategies of resistance. Such power of presence has been apparent in the chants, banners, jewelry, songs, slogans, and, most importantly, graffiti (an already overstudied means of expression).

The new text of the Revolution, in its different manifestations, has archived the anger and protests; it has also served as memory storage bank. What is remarkable about the new text is that it never presented a monolithic epistemic vision of gender; it was definitely far from that. In addition to reflecting different political positions of women, similar to the body, the new text performed gender in the most contested way. Against the backdrop of the aesthetic discourse imposed by the former regime, the new text reveals its capacity to signify a new discourse of gender. Whether the new texts can stand as a tool for rereading gender in the post-Revolution era is questionable.

Chapter three relocates the new poetic voices in juncture with the Revolution as an event. Put differently, poetry is not a new genre either in the literary or cultural milieu. However, the rise of new (and young) women's voices that adopt a subjective feminist tone is remarkable. In this sense, the poem becomes a performative intervention in the public sphere. The new voices (with all the multiple connotations of voice) merge the private and public with the personal and political; thus, breaching and transgressing all taken-for-granted boundaries. They take issue with the father figure, whereas the mother is always questioned, as if almost on trial. Similar to the female body, the poem becomes a site of contesting identity politics where one poet, Sara Allam, laments the disappearance of God, or rather His death, in her volume *Doun athar li qobla* (Without a trace of a kiss). It is noteworthy that these new voices are bent on subverting the logic of power; some negotiate, while others just shock the reader. That is, they stage a discursive confrontation that exalts the display of multiple subject positions.

Chapter four details the meaning of the gender paradox: how the alleged rise of democracy brought along the deterioration of women's rights. Ever since the overthrow of the Mubarak regime, women's rights have been tied severely to the rapid sociopolitical transformations, only to discredit the concept of citizenry. Unfortunately, women's rights have always been played out on a slippery terrain where identity is used as a bargaining chip. What has made things worse is that the web of power relations does not take the form of direct oppression that calls for resistance. Other unexpected factors complicate the scene, and, perhaps, the most difficult one is the role of women themselves in reproducing and consolidating the multiple faces of patriarchy. While they have contributed to the escalating process of extreme polarization, they have also propagated the concept of 'docile bodies.'

Amid this complexity, the new revolutionary generation has been exerting incessant efforts to free the female body from the shackles of the multiple conflicting ideologies (Islamic, liberal, nationalist, and leftist). From 11 February, the female body immediately became a site of contest. It started as early as March 2011, and, like the soothsayer's warning to Julius Caesar, we repeat, "Beware the Ides of March." The huge women's march celebrating International Women's Day that turned ugly and the protesters who were forced to go through a series of virginity tests were defining moments. Body disciplining as a means of sociopolitical control started to be a systematic practice against women protesters. While physical abuse and torture of men was interpreted as political, all forms of abuse practiced on women's bodies were taken to be cultural and, thus, acceptable. Michel Foucault explains that the purpose of employing the body as a means of discipline and punishment is to produce "subjected and practiced bodies, 'docile bodies.'"[10] However, Foucault treats the experiences of the human body as if there is no difference between men and women. One should ask how the disciplinary practices engender the bodies of women. Put differently, the harassed body is the means by which gender becomes "performative," as Judith Butler explains.[11] Reading the strategies by which the gendered violence was transformed by women into a means of subversion and resistance reveals how the route to exercising agency was paved. Conditions that were constraining and enslaving were turned around to be experienced as liberating and transforming—another paradox.

Chapter five investigates the politics of memory in its different forms: collective, political, and social. For the last twenty years, gender scholarship in Egypt has been working on the inclusion of women's voices, histories (*her*-story), and works into the 'official' hegemonic record (*his*-story). These efforts of forming a countermemory have been manifested in several fields: literature, textbooks, history, art, and research. In academia, rewriting history from the perspective of gender has flourished and has started to have an impact by accumulation. These efforts have aimed at subverting the concept of canonization and including women in the cultural memory or, rather, rescuing them from oblivion. Cultural memory is mainly an issue of power distribution; it is "an act in the present by which individuals and groups constitute their identities by recalling a shared past on the basis of common, and therefore often contested, norms, conventions, and practices."[12] This chapter is concerned with the various forms of memory transactions that managed to engage with the hegemonic patriarchal narrative.

Yet, the efforts of carving space for women in the cultural memory were forcefully knocked. Erasing women from the cultural memory and all forms of archive, accompanied by the discursive practices that twist women's position, fueled the struggle over memory. That is to say, what the culture remembers and what it chooses to forget or erase became a contested space (similar to the body and arts). This chapter investigates how reviving memory—whether identity related or that of violations—has become a powerful confrontational tool. In addition, the chapter highlights the forms of revival through which women could declare their position vis-à-vis power and power relations. Banners, stickers, chants, slogans, photographs, video clips, and graffiti are different forms of memory transactions that managed to contest and discredit the hegemonic, patriarchal narrative of the whole Revolution.

That the discourses of gender positions have gone through a series of transformations renders reaching the 'in conclusion' paragraph impossible. What starts as a process never concludes; gender is a construct that is claimed incessantly by all political powers, easily co-opted under the consent of those who are in power and in complicity with those who are not. And it is always bargained with by the father figure, the patriarch, or the national leader. Therefore, gender has the ability to transform, maneuver, resist, mobilize, and protest. The ongoing process of self-development and self-modification constitutes the narrative of gender, the history of women, and, thus, the narrative of the Revolution. While the history of nationalism in Egypt has involuntarily triggered the history of the women's movement, the rise and fall (and then rise again?) of gender since 2011 compels us to say that the narrative of women's experience forms the backbone of the Revolution narrative. The multiple, contradictory, relational, and situational gender positions formulate a method of approach to unravel the complicated and sometimes incomprehensible interaction of sociopolitical discourses. The belief that the slogan and chant "al-thawra mustamirra" (the revolution continues) means that it is not the time yet to say, "in conclusion." Thus, refraining from reaching a conclusion is a sign that there is yet a better future to come, and the future always supports the younger, fresh voices. There would be space to win, and for this to happen, we would need to lose it, then fight to restore it. Autumn is always followed by winter. In his poem "Ode to the West Wind," Percy Bysshe Shelley, the nineteenth-century Romantic and revolutionary poet, evoked the west wind (who we assume is female) and said:

> Wild Spirit, which art moving everywhere;
> Destroyer and Preserver; hear, O, hear!
> [. . .]
> Drive my dead thoughts over the universe
> Like withered leaves to quicken a new birth!
> And, by the incantation of this verse,
>
> Scatter, as from an unextinguished hearth
> Ashes and sparks, my words among mankind!
> Be through my lips to unwakened Earth
>
> The trumpet of a prophecy! O Wind,
> If Winter comes, can Spring be far behind?

1 IS THERE GENDER IN THIS REVOLUTION?

The Road to 2011

On 20 March 2003, the antiwar movement, specifically against Egypt's involvement in Iraq, escalated, and protesters took to Tahrir Square. For two days, the generation of the 1970s (Students' Movement) recalled several memories related to their movement through songs and chants, while a new generation was being chased by the security forces. Among the latter, women were the main actors. On 15 March 2005, Nafisa al-Marakbi (thirty-eight years old), a farmer from Sarando, a remote village in the Delta, died while defending her land against the capitalist tycoons. The whole village was besieged by police, and she was among those arrested, was beaten brutally in the police station, and died shortly after her release. On 21 March, the general prosecutor declared that al-Marakbi had died from natural causes and not because of physical torture. This story was repeated toward the end of 2010 when a young man, Khaled Said, died in a police station in Alexandria due to brutal physical torture. This time, the general prosecutor declared that he had died because he swallowed a marijuana joint. What was alarming in the latter incident was that Said was arrested, or rather abducted, on the grounds of a civil charge, not a political one. Between the two incidents of al-Marakbi and Said, anger had been escalating, and gender was an essential factor in the amalgam of protesting voices. In December 2006, Wedad al-Demerdash, a worker in Ghazl al-Mahalla Textile Factory, started a strike, along with three other women, demanding profit bonuses. Three days later, the men joined the strike. Hossam el-Hamalawy, a member of the Revolutionary Socialist Party, reported that "three thousand women garment workers struck and marched into the company compound demanding their male colleagues join their strike. The factory was brought to a complete halt, and for three days the area was the scene of marches and demonstrations."[1] Among the demands of al-Demerdash and her colleagues was equality of wages with men. These examples, and there are hundreds of similar ones, prove that gender has always played a role in inciting and sometimes leading protests in the political scene. Gender was not the possession of feminist nongovernmental organizations (NGOs) and, thus, was not confined to the narrow definition of 'rights' as advanced by educated, middle-class women. However, of importance is how gender conflates with other factors: class, ideology, and religion. That both al-Marakbi and Said died as a result of brutal torture is a fact that, ironically and sadly, testifies to the concept of equality in injustice. It also functions as a reminder of one of the precursors of the 2011 Revolution in the form of Asmaa Mahfouz's call to action in her blog.[2] These examples are not inclusive by any means; but they illustrate the point that women have been politically active since long before the Revolution. We must, therefore, sharpen the discourse about women's participation in the 2011 Revolution.

During the famous eighteen days (25 January to 11 February), Tahrir Square and the other squares across Egypt were the focus of, and were zoomed in on by, international television channels. The presence of women was evident and needed no further proof, whether watching events on TV or being present as an eyewitness—it was a simple fact that they were there. Yet, Arab and foreign media—and, of course, analysts and observers—dealt with this presence as a totally novel and unprecedented phenomenon. The role of women in the Revolution became a cliché that, surprisingly, was met with no objection. The unsaid in this cliché implies that Egyptian women have always been absent from the sociopolitical scene of the country, and, therefore, their presence deserves to be studied and understood. Many feminist activists and scholars have been asked to comment on the role of

Egyptian women in the Revolution, either in the media or in conferences and public events. Moreover, the obsession of the Western media with the conspicuous presence of women in the Revolution and its aftermath has salvaged a rubric from the 1980s and 1990s; it is that of Middle Eastern women and Muslim women. Needless to say, the events of 2011 and 2012 in the Arab World consolidated the latter label. In an eye-opening conversation between Lila Abu-Lughod and Rabab El-Mahdi, the problem of the discourse adopted by the Western media toward the participation of women in the Revolution was one of the main issues. El-Mahdi explains that this obsession obliterated the real presence of women in the sociopolitical scene long before the 2011 Revolution. She says:

> It dismisses the role that female workers have played in the wave of labor mobilization since 2006, the role of female activists in the pro-democracy and anti-war movements since 2003, and their constant presence in the student movement, just to name a few. Second, it assumes a level of gender-specificity that I am uncomfortable with; it is expecting that "women" are a homogenous group that would have a specific role in the revolution, disregarding the fact that different groups of women might participate differently depending on their locations (both geographic and class-based).[3]

El-Mahdi's strong logic could be easily discerned by any scholar or activist in the field. This makes the question more persistent: Why was it taken for granted by the media that women's participation is something new? The answer to this question must grapple with the policy of the ex-regime in dealing with women's issues and rights. To render all Egyptian people as a homogenous group was one of the goals of the Mubarak regime, since such a rendition increased control and produced a specific image of stability, not to mention the fact that it hid the major issues that needed to be addressed. In other words, Egypt merited only a fantasy of diversity, propagated by state policies, especially those related to the positioning of women. As a typical Third World regime, the authoritarian elites[4] vehemently deployed the ill-famed essential rhetoric about homogenous communities that provides positive images in order to construct a specific image of the nation. This nonexisting homogeneity allowed the regime to exercise more power and control. Yet, subverting this constructed image was an ongoing process. Therefore, as McClintock says, nations are not "simply phantasmagoria of the mind," but "they are historical practices through which social difference is both invented and performed." Among these differences, gender stands as one of the main constituents of identity, and this explains why the ex-regime was so concerned with controlling and legitimizing a certain system of gender as the dominant cultural representation; that is, it "amounted to the sanctioned institutionalization of gender difference" by enforcing state feminism.[5]

State Feminism: What Is It Good For?

That state feminism, led by ex-first lady Suzanne Mubarak, co-opted the concept of 'women's rights' is not without its consequences. Women's rights became part of the Mubarak regime; in fact, the 'woman question' has since become part and parcel of any regime. This is because the Personal Status Law has always been ordained and modified by the state; the modifications, however, never mirrored the actual progress of the feminist movement. Yet, any modification has always been discerned by society as a legacy of the state. Thus, we hear of "Suzanne's Laws" and "Gihan [Sadat]'s Laws"; that is, any modifications have always been tied to the name of the first lady, a fact that facilitated the crackdown on the law later. The situation becomes complicated when we realize that the state has always used women's rights—especially the Personal Status Law—as a terrain for bargaining. The law was used as a tool for propagating women's rights, insofar as it pertained to the project of modernism, and, at the same time, it was used to enforce patriarchal conservative values that allowed for more social control.

Since women's rights have always been linked to the project of building the modern state, they have never achieved legitimacy on the ground. At the same time, the work of activists was appropriated and manipulated by 'official' representatives. If we add to all the above how the ex-regime homogenized women (and men as well) to propagate an unreal image of the country, we can understand the extreme hostility toward women and their rights in the period that followed the ousting of Mubarak. The first shocking and hostile reaction to the woman question took place on

8 March 2011. A demonstration celebrating International Women's Day was attacked and harassed verbally by the crowds. Again, the media was obsessed with the way the demonstration turned ugly, and the headlines described what happened as a shocking blow. It was shocking and it took a while to understand the reason behind such hostility and aggression. Women's rights, simply, had been tied to the name of Suzanne Mubarak and the ex-regime. In a telling interview, Hoda Elsadda states that one of the main obstacles women's rights activists are bound to encounter is

> a prevalent public perception that associates women's rights activists and activities with the ex-First Lady, Suzanne Mubarak and her entourage, that is with corrupt regime politics. This public perception is already being politically manipulated to rescind laws and legislative procedures that were passed in the last ten years to improve the legal position of women, particularly within Personal Status Laws (PSL). These laws are deliberately being discredited as "Suzanne's laws."[6]

What happened on 8 March is interpreted differently by El-Mahdi. Her different approach reflects her ideology that takes issue with the whole project of the concept of women's rights. In answer to a question posed by Abu-Lughod about what the various groups of women are doing politically in the light of the "NGO-ization of women's rights work," El-Mahdi replies:

> Unlike those who would like to interpret this low turnout as revealing a lack of support for women's rights, I found this lack of response very telling about the extent to which these organizations and individuals are detached from society. Even the symbolism of choosing the date (March 8th), which has no significance for most Egyptian women, and the call for a march that made no specific demands except the "rights of women," is revealing. It is as if there is a set of rights that one can demand, devoid of context and position. This non-specificity made "women's rights" vulnerable to attack as "Western" or foreign.[7]

The problem with the above analysis is that it refuses categorically any link to the global politics of feminism, despite that transnational feminism is a strong form of solidarity and of founding common ground without losing specificity. At the same time, this utter dismissal of any global coloring negates the idea of multiplicity El-Mahdi defends throughout the conversation.

The fragile position of women's rights in Egypt stems from the strategies of the state, as practiced by the ex-regime of Mubarak. They are strategies that alienated society toward the concept itself and brought it down to a reductionist definition of gender equality. The main concern of the ex-regime was to deny the existence of any problems that might tarnish the image of Egyptian women. Violence against women, in both the private and public spheres, was utterly denied, and when it became part of the agenda as set by international concerns, the regime had to change its discourse, though naïvely. The official representatives resorted to reminding the audience of Islam's teachings and bringing up examples of violence against women that took place in the United States to prove that it was a universal phenomenon.

The obsession of the ex-regime (and the ones before) with producing a homogenous, positive image of women resulted in excluding all the dissenting, different feminist voices, along with their supporters and labeling them as the 'other.' That is to say, they are classified as those who are trying to deform the image of the nation and sabotage the national project. Deniz Kandiyoti has called this process of inclusion and exclusion "utopian populism"; that is, social unity is achieved on the grounds of agreeing on the position of women, as the cornerstone of cultural authenticity. The politics of authenticity are usually very complicated, where the West is presented as the Other. Yet, Kandiyoti perceives the problem as a much broader one, since the representations of that Other take very different forms. She explains that

anti-imperialistic pronouncements about the West are often a thinly disguised metaphor to articulate disquiet about more proximate causes for disunity. These include the existence of indigenous social classes with different cultural orientations and conflicting interests, and the coexistence of religiously and ethnically diverse collectivities in the very bosom of the nation. Discourses on women's authenticity are therefore at the heart of a utopian populism which attempts to obliterate such divisions by demarcating the boundaries of the 'true' community and excluding the 'Other within.'[8]

Utopian populism, heavily and systematically exercised by the ex-regime in relation to activists' work and voices (and also other things), rendered the conflation between women's rights and a discredited regime inevitable. This is one of the main reasons that endowed post-Revolution Egypt with a paradox that subverts the paradigm of democracy. State policies, especially those related to women's positioning, propagated a fantasy of diversity by denying the charge of exclusion. As a typical Third World regime, the authoritarian elites have vehemently deployed the ill-famed essential rhetoric about homogenous national communities (reminiscent of Benedict Anderson's "imagined communities"[9]) and positive images in order to construct a specific image of the nation. That popular unity was one of the reasons that led to suppressing the different forms of the subject's agency. On the road to the 2011 Revolution, women's rights became a marker of a corrupt authoritarian regime.

Thus, the hostility that started from March 2011 can be understood. The main problem is that women's rights and the woman question, in their various transformations, have always been tied to the politics of nationalism.

The Marriage of Nationalism and Gender

The long historical entanglement of women's rights issues in ideological, national, and political struggles is the foundation of all the ensuing politics that supported or discredited the citizenship of women. In her book that focuses on the Egyptian women's movement, Nadje Al-Ali states that

feminist projects in anti-colonial struggles have often been sacrificed to the cause of national liberation and, in the aftermath of independence, women have been relegated to their former 'domestic' roles. However, there were points of convergence between nationalist and feminist struggles, especially when the nation was envisioned as 'modern.'[10]

The most flagrant example we have seen in the Arab World is what happened to Algerian women. Once independence was obtained, all the women were ordered to go back home to perform their sacred duties. The public sphere came under the possession of men. It was the time of building the nation, and women's rights were not a priority, since there were more urgent issues. Leila Abouzeid has dealt with this issue in depth in her novel *Year of the Elephant*. In Abouzeid's book, Zahra, who supported the Revolution and worked undercover instead of her husband so as to protect him from being arrested, was immediately thrown onto the street after independence, because her husband replaced her with a 'modern' woman who could cope with the new era. He had simply sat down and said to her, "'Your papers will be sent to you along with whatever the law provides.' My papers? How worthless a woman is if she can be returned with a paper receipt like some store-bought object! How utterly worthless!"[11]

Kumari Jayawardena's seminal book *Feminism and Nationalism in the Third World*[12] has detailed the entanglement of both concepts in the nineteenth and early twentieth centuries. The book has served as one of the essential and necessary references in documenting and analyzing women's movements in the Third World. Despite the fact that the book has become a classic by now, its importance stems from the fact that it debunks the idea that feminism was imported from the West. However, it also reveals the fact that feminism started with national struggles to build a modern nation. That is, feminism has always been contoured and controlled by the ebbs and flows of political struggles and trajectories—hence, the limitations of nationalism. The women's movement in Egypt stands at the heart of this paradigm, where the woman question was born with the 1919 Revolution. And, ever since that time, women's rights have never managed to stand independent of the competing discourses of the state, Islamists, and nationalists. The history of the Egyptian women's movement could be read in the history of modern Egypt and, of course, vice versa. Many valuable studies have dealt with this history that usually takes the end of nineteenth century as its point of departure, that is, with the publication of Qasim Amin's debut books *The Liberation of Women* (1899), followed by *The New Woman* (1900). Kandiyoti, Beth Baron, Mervat Hatem, Nadje Al-Ali, and Leila Ahmed,[13] to name but a few, have rendered detailed analyses of the history and trajectory of the Egyptian women's movement and the interaction of feminism with nationalism and Islamism.

From the very beginning, although beginnings are hard to find, the woman question was among the markers of identity. Put differently, from very early on, it was at the mercy of identity politics. Although the invitation that Huda Shaarawi received to attend the conference of the International Women's Union in Rome incited her to call for the formation of the Association of the Egyptian Women's Union in March 1923, the constitution of 1923 came out in April without any trace of women's demands in its 170 articles. Hala Kamal notes that

> when the post-revolution constitution was issued in 1923, women's demands were not met. Article 3 of the 1923 Constitution stated: "Egyptians shall be equal before the law in enjoying civil and political rights, and in public duties and mandates, with no discrimination among them therein on the grounds of origin, language or religion" (Dostoor, 1923). Thus, the first Egyptian constitution ignored women's rights, while it recognized the ethnic and religious diversity characteristic of the Egyptian society, by establishing equality and rejecting ethnic as well as religious discrimination.[14]

So the building of the nation meant excluding women from such an important document. With different levels of intensity, the battle of inserting women's rights in the constitution (in 1923, 1930, 1934, 1935, 1952, 1953, 1956, 1958, 1962, 1964, and 1971) continued. However, the 2011 Revolution made it seem certain that, among other things, the phrasing of women's rights in the constitution was bound to change in order to mirror reality or at least mirror what happened in Tahrir Square. Yet, such an expectation was not met at all, and women were not even properly represented in the assembly that was formed by the Morsi government to draft the constitution.

With the formation of the 2012 Parliament, it was very obvious that Islamism had replaced nationalism[15] in the power struggle to control the position of women's rights. Article 10 in that constitution says:

> The family is the basis of the society founded on religion, morality and patriotism. The State is keen to preserve the genuine character of the Egyptian family, its cohesion and stability, and to protect its moral values, all as regulated by law. The State shall ensure maternal and child health services free of charge, and enable the reconciliation between the duties of a woman toward her family and her work. The State shall provide special care and protection to female breadwinners, divorced women and widows.[16]

The amount of problems and controversies this article leads to are huge, yet "the genuine character of the Egyptian family" is the most ambiguous and controversial part. What is the genuine character of a social entity, the family, in this case? Who decides the criteria? And most importantly, why is it "character" and not "characters"? Inherent in the phrasing of this article is the concept of a homogenous community, "founded on religion, morality and patriotism." The dismissal of diversity, along with singling out "divorced women" and "widows," was an alarming sign in relation to the sociopolitical perception of women's position in a country as large as Egypt.

Women continued to be taken as the transmitters and producers of the national culture, which meant they were denied agency by being forced politically and discursively to conform to a monolithic image and a gendered discourse that overlooked all sociopolitical and cultural differences. McClintock explains the process:

> Excluded from direct action as national citizens, women are subsumed symbolically into the national body politic as its boundary and metaphoric limit: . . . . Women are typically construed as the symbolic bearers of the nation, but are denied any direct relation to national agency.[17]

Perceived as the iconic representation of culture and the marker of national boundaries, women experienced physically, discursively, and symbolically all forms of violence related to the denial of agency. Replacing gender with the family meant an obliteration of any specificity of women's issues and rendered sex and gender indistinct. Even with the occurrence of the word "protect" twice in this article, women were patronized and chastised on the streets, an act that sometimes amounted to violence.

The dismissal of any diversity, and replacing "women" with "woman," ignited a severe process of polarization, and, again, the word "women" was used to declare identity. To be more accurate, in 2013, women were used to declare the building of a modern country.[18] The 2011 Revolution revealed the fact that there are several constructs of gender; simultaneously, we have to rethink the formation of gender and its relation to the concept of nationalism. However, the complicated web of power relations co-opted women, only to relocate them as markers of cultural and ideological identity. Amid this mishmash of conflicting political players, the poignant link between feminism and nationalism comes to the fore. Recently, nationalism has been displayed in, for example, the unequivocal support of the military (for the sake of national security) and the deep polarization carried out and perpetrated on women (for the sake of cultural identity). In this wide spectrum of interpretations and representations, we can hear voices that really struggle to disentangle women's rights from nationalism, which is in itself a changing, unfixed concept: sometimes it is directed against neocolonialism, and in 2015, it is directed against the ideological other. Due to this high-pitched tone of nationalism (that comes close to chauvinism), the space for lobbying for and supporting women's rights is almost completely eroded. That is why hope in the future remains in the rising generation with its unique voice that goes beyond gender without abandoning it. The vision expressed by this voice requestions nationalism and redefines gender constructs. The redefinition is definitely not discursive, but, rather, it comes through the actions and reactions toward the daily micropolitics of women's life. It is a voice charged with the consciousness that identity is flexible and changing and that the quest for authenticity means nothing—if there is anything in the first place that could be called 'authentic.'

Women's Agency

According to humanist theorists, agency is synonymous with being a person, the free and autonomous individual. The conventional account of humanism emphasizes the self as something homogenous, unified, rational, in possession of consciousness and moral authority, and separate from the world around it. Descartes's and Immanuel Kant's theories revolve around this self. Such a definition has its limitations and cannot generate any reading or understanding of the individual (along with collectives) who rebels against the system, makes choices, changes his or her discursive position, suffers from fragmentation and discontinuity, redresses interruption by resorting to negotiations, and seeks the grafting of identity to new subject positions. Poststructuralist theory, developed in large part as an opposition to humanist theory, helps to understand the subject positions and the agency—allowed or hindered—that the Egyptian sociopolitical arena has witnessed since 2011. An example clarifies this: In 2011, women were one of the main political players who populated Tahrir Square; that their presence was not welcomed after that is part of the narrative. Again, they were part of the protests against the Supreme Council of Armed Forces (SCAF), and I hasten to add that the only lawyer who managed to attend the investigations of those arrested by the military was a woman.[19] In the presidential elections of 2012 (the quandary of voting for either Ahmed Shafiq or Mohamed Morsi in the final run-off), photos of women queuing for long hours in front of the poll stations swamped the media. A year later, 2013, women were out on the streets protesting against Morsi, and, later, they were the main supporters of General Abdel Fattah al-Sisi—they were, in fact, dancing and ululating in front of the same poll stations. The conclusion from this is that Egyptian women presented an incomprehensible phenomenon to all observers. No media or political analysts could explain these radical shifts, from Mubarak to Morsi to al-Sisi, from autocracy to Islamism to militarism. This example is important because it functions as one of the main factors of the big narrative of the Revolution, which is agency. We can never understand what really happened without the help of poststructuralist theory. In *Mappings*, Susan Stanford Friedman explains that agency does not mean "autonomy or freedom to act"; according to her poststructuralist and thorough analysis of locational feminism, she defines agency as "the assumption of human subjectivities that create meanings and act in negotiation with the systemic conditions of the social order, however circumscribed."[20] Or as Julian Henriques puts it, the self is not separate from the collective and the social context, "the subject itself is the effect of a production, caught in the mutually constitutive web of social practices, discourses and subjectivity, its reality is the tissue of social relations."[21] One makes possible choices from those available. The whole process of agency is governed by negotiation, which means that the same subject could experience multiple positions. Bronwyn Davies states that in contrast to agency in the humanist theory, where any adult and sane person has a unified and rational identity, agency and experience in post-structuralist theory have different meanings. It does not revolve around identity; it is rather all about experience, which is

> captured in the notion of *subjectivity*. Subjectivity is constituted through those *discourses* in which the person is being positioned at any one point in time, both through their own and others' acts of speaking/writing. One discourse that contradicts another does not undo one's constitution in terms of the original discourse. One's subjectivity is *therefore necessarily contradictory*. It is also to some extent outside of or larger than those aspects of being that come under rational or conscious control.[22]

According to the above excerpt, Egyptian women had to negotiate the best choices available in specific political situations. Such choices come closer to forced choices, since the subject positioning within particular discourses (Morsi or Shafiq) makes the chosen action the only possible (and perhaps best) one. This does not mean that it is the only choice (if so, then the idea of choice is annihilated), but, rather, because the position of the subject in this discourse makes this choice the only one possible. In this case, the revolutionary discourse and the will to demolish the old regime rendered voting for Morsi the best choice. On par with that is the large group who decided not to vote at all, by way of a boycott. In both cases, the exercise of power exists. Yet, it is not the power of violence that dominates. Michel Foucault never perceived the subject as a preexisting autonomous thing that power oppressed. Instead, he believes that modern power operates by defining the ways through which a person can become a subject.[23]

The New Geographics of Identity

The 2011 Revolution, therefore, contoured new geographics of identity, where the poststructuralist feminist subject exercised agency. As mentioned earlier, different and sometimes contradictory discourses guided women's subject positioning—a fact that imbued their choices with ambiguity and ambivalence. However, class, religion, location, the past, the present, coalitions, solidarity, knowledge, and gender informed the choices made by women. All together, these formed the new geographics of identity. Friedman states that, instead of "the individualistic telos of developmental models" (after the humanist theory), this new geographics

> figures identity as a historically embedded site, a positionality, a location, a standpoint, a terrain, an intersection, a network, a crossroads of multiply situated knowledges. It articulates not the organic unfolding of identity but rather the mapping of territories and boundaries, the dialectical terrains of inside/outside or center/margin, the axial intersections of different positionalities, and the spaces of dynamic encounter—"the contact zone," the "middle ground," the borderlands, *la frontera*.[24]

This is the epistemological foundation of the new geographics; it is not confined to one place or one position; neither is it related to a certain power. It goes to and fro, and, in this constant movement, it explores new possibilities and holds them open for the future. In its attempt to start afresh, it also carves new spaces for action, invents new strategies of resistance, and weaves new discourses of identity. It is fully aware of "the lack of solid ground, the ceaseless change of fluidity," and, thus, it is always in flight from fixed interpretations or judgments. The new geographics of identity makes use of the local and global in a 'glocal' way; it adapts "the landscapes of accelerating change, the technologies of information highways."[25]

While the definition of the new geographics almost describes the forms of actions taken by women, the content of their choices and the politics of subject positioning should be examined. What were these choices based on? What could justify unexpected transversal coalitions? Where had the homogenous image of women gone? Why and how did gender—as a factor of analysis—change its place in situations and contexts that used to be interpreted solely through gender? Why would a non-Islamist woman elect an Islamist president? Why were the attempted answers to these questions, and similar others, mostly erroneous and far from reality? Perhaps, we need to look at the common approaches that have long been employed to read women's position in general and in the Egyptian Revolution in particular. Long used in feminist literary studies, the practices of gynocriticism and gynesis,[26] advanced by Elaine Showalter in the 1980s, have been the lens through which women's agency and subjectivity have been read and analyzed in the revolutions of the Arab World in general. If 'gynocriticism' means the study of women writers as a distinct literary tradition, studying the precursors of the women's movement is the equivalent in the general analysis of the Egyptian scene. And, if 'gynesis' means reading the discursive effect of the feminine, the equivalent is reading about the presence of women in the public sphere. As a response to the new revolutionary context in Egypt and the Arab World, the international and regional discourse about feminism worked under the general umbrella of 'the role of women in the Arab Spring.' In addition to reproducing another homogenous community of women, this approach does not pay attention to the polemics of the new geographics of identity. That is why the media could not go beyond the binary of Islamist and liberal (although 'liberalism' is a term that has originated in the discipline of economy).

Friedman suggests six discourses of identity that could be discerned and read in the new geography of positionalities.[27] They were developed sequentially in response to the fluid political landscapes, and they can appear multiply and simultaneously in spite of their different histories and influences. Friedman proposes them as "provisional schematization not as a taxonomy."[28] They only help to read the different positionalities. The first of these discourses appeared in the 1970s and 1980s and figures feminist identity as "multiple oppression."[29] It stresses the differences among women and takes oppression as the main constituent of identity, which leads to naming other kinds of victimization (class, religion, color, etc.). While piling up forms of oppression could be a weak point, this discourse has its own strength in the dialectical analysis. That is, oppression generates its antithesis, which is power. The second discourse on positionality—during the mid to late 1980s—assumes that identity is the site of multiple subject positions and a product of interdependent systems of alterity. To explain, because the self is not singular (like the self of humanism), it is not enough to say 'Muslim women.' There must be other parameters related to the location that the self occupies. Unlike the discourse of multiple oppression, this discourse does not focus on oppression but on the multifarious combinations of difference that might and might not include oppression. The third discourse of identity, which appeared sporadically in the 1980s and became common in the 1990s, is the contradictory subject positions. This is one of the common positionalities the Revolution has revealed. During Morsi's rule, for example, an Islamist woman could be privileged because of her ideology and oppressed because of her gender. A Coptic woman could be privileged because of her class and oppressed because of her religion. The fourth discourse of positionality is that of relationality. It appeared in the 1990s and consolidated the poststructuralist notion of subjectivity as multiple and contradictory. It introduced also the relationship between gender and other axes of identity. We have examples of this positionality during the eighteen days (25 January to 11 February). A black Egyptian woman trying to enter Tahrir Square could sometimes be taken as a foreigner and, thus, either welcomed or attacked. It depended on the gazer and the inspectors at the gate. The appearance of thousands of Coptic women was cheered by the crowd in the square, whereas they were vilified in the media as traitors. The different factors of identity function relationally as sites of inclusion or exclusion; it depends on the point of reference, the historical circumstances, and the conditions. The fifth discourse is situational; it focuses on the setting, and, thus, it is related to postcolonial studies. In 2014, the Rafah crossing between Gaza and Egypt was closed. Many people were angry, yet the majority approved of such an offensive measure[30]. In all cases, continuing the discussion with logic and minimum decency was impossible. Shortly after that, I traveled to Beirut to attend a seminar. And, much to my chagrin, I was held responsible and accountable for the closure only because I am Egyptian. Setting and place control, which constitute identity, are to be foregrounded.

The last discourse of positional identity is that of hybridity. It basically means "the cultural grafting that is the production of geographical migration."[31] While living between more than one culture is definitely a rich experience, it could also be a painful one. This discourse of identity has recently become one of the main constructs that influence the Egyptian sociopolitical scene. Immediately after the ousting of Mubarak, several Egyptians returned to the country with very ambitious plans for the new era. Much to their disappointment, the rhetoric they used was not very well received; neither did they know how to interact with the political scene. When the scene became more complicated, their opinions earned them the label 'traitors.' In a position paper about the consequences of militarizing Egypt through the unequivocal support of General al-Sisi, Nadje Al-Ali problematizes the issue of the insider/outsider. A long quote from that paper is useful, as it explains the whole situation:

> I was quite shocked by the initial reactions of some of my feminist friends and colleagues in Egypt, whose hatred of the Muslim Brotherhood seemed to have translated into an initially uncritical applauding of its violent suppression, as well as a glorification of the actions of the military as "the will of the people."
>
> Let me add here that I do feel uncomfortable about sitting in London and making recommendations to, or even worse passing judgment about, my feminist colleagues and friends in Egypt. I continue to feel humbled and profoundly impressed by their resourcefulness, commitment, and resolve. I am also deeply aware that things look different from the inside, and that it is always easier to have "principled" and righteous positions sitting in a safe haven in London or New York, or in Copenhagen, Stockholm or Oslo for that matter.

That things are often more complex than they might appear from the outside, I learnt in the context of my research and activism in relation to Iraq. I have lost several friends over the last few years whose anti-imperialist and anti-occupation positions translated into fierce criticism of feminist activists (or any other activist and intellectual for that matter) who participated in any political processes or transition instigated by either the occupation forces or a government lacking widespread legitimacy. For some of my friends in London, and elsewhere in the diaspora, those Iraqis who worked with the Iraqi government or engaged in any form of exchange with the occupation were traitors and were not to be trusted. My position was different and so I also became a traitor in the eyes of some, although I have always upheld my anti-occupation position. I just did not think that it was either fair or realistic to expect people inside the country, living under occupation and an undemocratic government, not to try to influence processes and developments.[32]

This quasi testimony, as much as it is painful, is an eye-opener. It brings attention to the dilemma of insider versus outsider—that is, the question of who is more loyal and faithful? Who is more eligible to analyze the situation? It is also a summing up of the utopian populism, where any different opinion that does conform to the norm is excluded. On the other side, the cliché "the will of the people"—if anybody can speak for the people—is a signifier of which the signified is the sum of the different positionalities, the quotidian details of confrontations, the harassed bodies, the disdain toward women, the fear of the future, and the collapse of the surrounding countries with women being sold as slaves—in short, the new geographics of identity. What also comes into play in this dilemma is the voice versus the unvoice (although not the issue of silence). The position of the United States and the West toward the ousting of Morsi by the military generated a binary that governs the political discourses—that is, was it a coup or a revolution? For a while, Egyptians were concerned with voicing their opinion to the Western media, and, thus, any different voice that had access to the foreign media and academia was considered an act of treason. Because the voice of the outsider (and hybrid) "intervenes, unsettles, interrogates, ironizes, denaturalizes, transgresses by refusing to 'fit' established categories," it was categorically interrupted and silenced.[33] This practice came close to the dictatorship of the majority, yet the voice of this majority was not heard; it was taken as a ubiquitous mania. Perhaps, Al-Ali, and many others, had to wait for events to settle and for the insider to be able to take a step back to get a clearer view in order to try to influence processes and development. Spatial and temporal conditions control the whole equation. Time was needed to shift agency to another level, to make other choices, and to be able to speak with authority. "Feminist, poststructuralist authority would not be coercive and would not be located within dominant discourses except insofar as it persuaded them to change themselves, to become more multiple, flexible and inclusive of different points of view," as Davies advises.[34]

Beyond Gender

In her project of going beyond gender, gynocriticism and gynesis in particular, Friedman is careful to explain what she means in order not to run the risk of implying that the word 'beyond' means a linear model of change that leaves behind initial formations. She advocates for "a palimpsestic view of changing critical practices, a spatialized metaphoric of history in which what has gone before synchronically remains, continuing to influence the new, however much it is itself subject to change."[35] In a nutshell, gender remains and was never abandoned. Doing away with gender, or even implying the idea, backgrounds women's agency, resistance, and power. Gender is an essential and legitimate category of analysis, and the material conditions that brought gynocriticism and gynesis into practice still exist. If the linear connotations of the word 'beyond' are appropriated by those who have always been indifferent to the woman question, gender can be displaced as an old-fashioned category that has to be replaced by more sophisticated terms. When it comes to fathoming the revolutionary (con)text, it is all too easy to claim that men and women were equal in receiving the bullets and that there is no need to single out or specify gender.

In spite of all the risks that lurk in the word 'beyond,' there must be a new approach—that includes and foregrounds gender—to reading the new geographics of identity and to understanding the substantial changes that have occurred politically, socially, and epistemologically. It is an approach that should not regard gender as a priori a fixed and essential category of analysis. According to Friedman, and in accordance with the trajectory of women in the Revolution, the approach to the narrative should be locational. It "incorporates diverse formations because its positional analysis requires a kind of geopolitical literacy built out of a recognition of how different times and places produce different and changing gender systems as these intersect with other different and changing societal stratifications and movements for social justice."[36] This locational feminist approach integrates the six discourses of positionality in order to render a narrative of the Revolution based on gender. Of importance as well is that it requires a geopolitical literacy that acknowledges the interaction of the local and the global; a requirement that does not imply the formula of universal oppression of women. It is a form of literacy that ensures one understands one's epistemological position so as to be able to exercise discursive agency. Finally, a geopolitical locational feminism

> travels globally in its thinking, avoiding the imposition of one set of cultural conditions on another, assuming the production of local agencies and conceptualization, and remaining attentive to the way these differences are continually in the process of modification through interactions within a global system of diverse, multidirectional exchanges.[37]

It is an approach that looks inside and outside to be able to make the best choice. In a very spontaneous manner, and, perhaps as the result of accumulated knowledge, feminist activists displayed high awareness of the geopolitical and glocal surroundings in the way they organized their collectives and strategies of resistance, especially those related to combating sexual harassment, in their lobbying, in their chants and slogans, and in all the action plans designed to protect agency and authority.[38] While these practices could be taken at face value as a series of reactions toward violations of women's rights and bodies, it is essential to remember that accumulation of knowledge and the testing of different discourses have sharpened the agency of women, even if the price was high. The experience women have gained is a form of agency itself, and their transversal coalition with other movements is a proof of the ability to make choices locationally.

Although this book is primarily concerned with the practices, voices, and agencies of the rising generation, it cannot, by any means, ignore the fact that without the achievements of a previous generation gender would not have had that high ranking importance in the epistemic view of activists and scholars. Is there gender in this Revolution? Definitely, there is. However, the dream-like atmosphere of the eighteen days rendered the necessity and specificity of gender nebulous. A utopia does not require approaches or strategies. That is why thanks are due to the dystopian scene that prevailed from a very early time (March 2011) and called for an explicit gender approach and discourse. Yet, it had to be locational, on the ground, in the streets, and in a ceaseless negotiation between focus on gender and sexual difference and "scrutiny of the multifaceted matrices in which gender is only one among many axes of identity."[39]

2 GENDER AND THE NEW TEXT

S ince the eruption of the Revolution, artistic expression has been hoisted to a higher rank. Technically, the use of a new language to express the revolt and protest became a point of attraction in the poetics of the Revolution. No research can ignore the new means of expression that generated what I term the new text. It is a text that has established a strong and novel relation with politics. Indeed, the Revolutionary event has benefited from this new aesthetic text by introducing itself as a radical event and a discursive shift in the whole paradigm. In other words, the Revolution has gained substantial flesh through the artistic expression that has become in itself a tool of protest and resistance. As Bill Ashcroft puts it: "The creative cultural product is unmatched in its ability to cultivate hope because creativity itself is the act of 'stepping beyond.'"[1]

However, taking into consideration the discourse of going beyond gender, as detailed in the previous chapter, it becomes a difficult task to speak about the gendered performance of art, though one can find a few examples that refer directly to a transformed construct of gender or, rather, a construct that was in the making. Whether these examples endured time and proliferated or faded away is questionable. Yet, it is an unforgettable fact that women and art were the two phenomena that attracted the attention of analysts, correspondents, and observers of the Egyptian Revolution. Moreover, gender was taken to have been revolutionized through reading, for example, the graffiti related to women. That was definitely a rash conclusion, far from accuracy, not to mention reality. Graffiti related to women was part and parcel of the revolutionary stance as a whole and not a separate subset of protest and revolution as identified by those from outside the movement. One can talk about works of art that backed up the language of protest and contributed to the binary of 'us' and 'them,' that has differentiated the position of protesters from that of the prevailing sensibility and dominant discourse.

What is the best way, then, to discuss the combination of art, gender, and the Revolution? Should it be something like the role of women and art in the Revolution? But women were not assigned a role; they were committed to a revolutionary act that was bent on demolishing the old sociopolitical structure, where men and women suffered equally, and, thus, social justice became the main demand. Yet, it was a revolution, an event in the world (to borrow the words of Edward Said[2]) of which women and art formed a big part. In other words, there was a unique specificity of the presence of women in the new aesthetic text that was inspired, in its turn, by the rising protest discourse and, therefore, signified—most probably unconsciously—a change in the way gender was constructed and perceived.

New Generation and New World

The new aesthetic text that was born out of the dynamics of the Revolution could serve as the basis for reading the changes (if there are any) that occurred in the process of constructing and understanding gender. This text had (and still has) different manifestations, where demands and protests have been documented and archived (even if erased or destroyed later). This new text never presented a monolithic epistemic vision about gender; it was definitely far from that. In addition to reflecting different political positions of women, the new text wrote, sprayed, drew, performed, and expressed gender in the most contested way. Against the backdrop of the familiar aesthetic discourse imposed and supported by the Mubarak regime, where gender emanated mainly from the discourse

of legal equality, I will explore the potentiality of the new text to signify new constructs of gender, where the discourse of legal equality is
transgressed. I will attempt to read how women—as part of the mobilized
citizenry—managed to rework the concept of identity and assert multiple
positions of subjectivity, through not only art but also a new established
relationship between art and politics, which is one of the most important
achievements of the Revolution. Can the new text(s) stand as a tool of
rereading gender in the post-Revolution context?

In addition to giving birth to a different mind-set, the 25 January
Revolution allowed for the eruption of differences[3] previously suppressed
through an incessant celebration of homogeneity. The outbreak of the
Revolution marked the appearance of a real diversity on several levels:
ideological, cultural, religious, educational, class-based, and gender-oriented. This diversity allowed for the rise of not only a new text but also
a new generation, whose consciousness comes close to (but is not iden-
tical with) the avant-garde, as detailed by Jurgen Habermas. The rising
Egyptian avant-garde "understands itself as invading unknown territory,
exposing itself to the dangers of sudden, shocking encounters, conquer-
ing an as yet unoccupied future."[4] It is a generation (a term not without its
reservations[5]) that has managed to weave its own political discourse vis-
à-vis a regressive discourse that I call *arrière-garde*.[6] The confrontation
becomes tenser because the latter is deeply rooted in the institutional,
social, economic, cultural, and political fabric of the country—what is
referred to in chapter four as 'the rhizomatic structure.'

The sociopolitical consciousness articulated in and by the avant-
garde practices and discourse is not ahistorical: "It is directed against
what might be called a false normativity in history."[7] It does not assume
any aesthetic Surrealist role or political Leninist position, as did the generation that Habermas dealt with; in fact, the Egyptian avant-garde is
not even aware of its position as a practice and discourse that functions
to shock the traditional bourgeois sense, a message constantly conveyed
in highly creative initiatives based on either new forms of expression or
new visions channeled through the old forms. Paradoxically, what endows
the avant-garde with power is that it does not seek power. It only seeks
social justice in its different manifestations; put differently, it seeks, after

the main chant of the Revolution, bread, liberty, and social justice.[8] This progressive spirit of the avant-garde continuously stages a dialectical play between the local and global; it is fascinated by the shock that accompanies the act of deconstructing all fixed local assumptions, and, yet, it is always in flight, fearful of falling for the global. Somehow, it is both anti-local and antiglobal. The conflict has gradually turned out to be between a new shocking revolutionary discourse, with gender included but not centralized, that strives to demolish old structures categorically and a discourse adopted by the majority that yearns for stability, where old fixed norms are glorified and recalled nostalgically.

As part of that new rising discourse, women revolted against a fake normative image of modernism where their niche was contoured and defined by external powers. The strong national discourse of a patriarchal state—former and current—disseminated and propagated a fixed image of gender that considered women to be the markers of identity of the nation.[9] In exploring the awkward relation between gender and nationalism, Deniz Kandiyoti has stated that

> cultural nationalism is typically animated by the contradictory logic of popular sovereignty and the expansion of citizenship rights, on the one hand, and the reaffirmation of authentic cultural values, on the other, assigning women an ambiguous position by defining them both as co-citizens and as the privileged custodians of national values. This ambiguity often lies at the heart of women's inability to achieve the status of fully enfranchised citizens.[10]

The fixity of the image, along with the ethical power it exercised in the field of art, resulted in the marginalization of a large sector of women and the delimitation of multiple and diverse positionalities, for the sake of prioritizing 'authentic' cultural values. Therefore, the rise of the avant-garde meant the rise of women and led to the formation of new positions of subjectivity displayed transversally and aesthetically in alternative contested spaces. Women's struggle to constitute and sustain discursive and institutional networks that deconstruct the arrière-garde's mind-sets is based on what Cornel West calls "demystification," and it is where the avant-garde tries to keep track of the complex dynamics of institutional and other related power structures in order to disclose options and alternatives for transformative praxis; it also attempts to grasp the way in which representational strategies are creative responses to novel circumstances and conditions. In this way the central role of human agency (always enacted under circumstances not of one's choosing)—be it in the critic, artist, or constituency, and audience—is accented.[11]

In such a new world, art becomes one of the most vital and effective micropolitical practices. For more accuracy, we should refer to the combination of art and revolution, in other words, art and politics. The implication here is far different from the slogan of 'every person is an artist' or 'life is art.' Such slogans, when adopted by society, function as a safety valve to alleviate the level of anger. Moreover, any instrumental normalizing relation between politics and art results in a totalizing discourse where individualization is deleted and the default frame of mind is restored. Walter Benjamin has discussed this extensively in his article "The Work of Art in the Age of Mechanical Reproduction"[12] and has detailed how a work of art loses its halo when reproduced by the masses. Therefore, my focus is on the rise of the new aesthetic text that was a corollary of the rise of the new woman as part of the new generation.

The New Transversal Text

The new aesthetic text suggests a different relation between art and politics or, rather, the Revolution. It is a relation that manifests itself in practices that spring from every place, with no center and no production of replicas. At the same time, it is a threatened text, because it carries within the potential to fail, since activist art and aesthetic activism are continually persecuted by the state apparatus. It emerges in the cracks, the in-betweens, and at the most unexpected times, yet it cannot be documented in a linear fashion at all. In this text, there is no hierarchy either for art or the Revolution. The transversal nature of protests fulfills the concept investigated in depth by Gerald Raunig, where he prefers to use the term "concatenation" of art and politics instead of "connection."[13]

The new text transforms the relation between art and politics from instrumental to transversal[14] and demolishes the traditional hierarchy that turns art into a mere supporting factor of a specific political discourse. The new texts, in their various forms and genres, incur temporary overlaps between art and politics in a way that makes them, in Raunig's words,

> micropolitical attempts at the transversal concatenation of art machines and revolutionary machines, in which both overlap, not to incorporate one another, but rather to enter into a concrete exchange relationship for a limited time.[15]

The term was more developed when Félix Guattari focused more, in his activist work, on how modes of transversality "might produce different forms of (collective) subjectivity that break down oppositions between the individual and the group."[16] The idea was elaborated more by Michel Foucault, who suggested that these forms of connection shatter the alienation that power has worked so hard to insinuate.[17] Obviously, Guattari was critiquing the inherited forms of political organizations as 'the party,' and apparently, the majority of the new rising generation has realized that the ceiling of political parties is much lower than their aspirations. For practicality, I am using the term 'transversal' here to describe new terrains of open cooperation between activist, artistic, social, and political practices. Such new alliances, even if temporary, set to deterritorialize the disciplines and fields they work across. Transversality is not a form or an institution that one joins, but, rather, it is continuously constituted through events that require and trigger certain acts of alliance where art and the Revolution connect. It is important to state that these alliances could be temporary—that is to say, the alliances do not necessarily indicate the same political belonging. This explains how the new text makes its appearance in a demonstration against the Protest Law of 2013 or against sexual harassment or against a religious fatwa or against an old calcified discourse. It might appear—often abruptly—in all those spaces as an ally whose mission is to augment the message.

Transversality, thus, endows the new texts with the power of the popular (whose position is always perceived as dubious) to subvert the so-called highbrow culture (perceived as prestigious, official, and trust-worthy), especially the bourgeois traditional culture that has helped all forms of power (whether Islamic or not) to consolidate their own values. The deeply ingrained conceptions of what Egyptian society has come to call 'the correct behavior,' a weird and misleading concern in itself, have always been propagated and even strengthened by the traditional forms of art, and, naturally, they enjoyed the protection of the state. The Revolution, in all its stages, ups and downs, has certainly generated a new language that derives its power and credibility from popular culture. It is the language of protest and dissent that articulated itself through new syntax, creative means of expression, and uninstitutional places and deserted spaces. However, the most important thing is that the content channeled through this language is highly radical and revolutionary. Sub-versive as it is, the new text with its new language is neither embraced nor endorsed by the state. It remains all the time in the margin as "a space of weak power, but it is a space of power," Stuart Hall comments. He justi-fies this by saying:

> Anybody who cares for what is creatively emergent in the con-temporary arts will find that it has something to do with the languages of the margin, and this trend is increasing. New subjects, new genders, new ethnicities, new regions, and new com-munities—all hitherto excluded from the major forms of cultural representation, unable to locate themselves except as decentered or subaltern—have emerged and have acquired through strug-gle, sometimes in very marginalized ways, the means to speak for themselves for the first time. And the discourses of power in our society, the discourses of the dominant regimes, have been certainly threatened by this decentered cultural empowerment of the marginal and local.[18]

That this new text expresses and stems from different positionalities banished for a long time in the margins not only endows it with power but also qualifies it to be a tool of analysis, capable of interpreting an important part of the sociopolitical situation. By default, women are situated in the center of that situation; that is, their position is, more often than not, the marker of the itinerary of the Revolution. Therefore, "marginality has become a powerful space" in the dynamic interplay of local and global.[19]

Instead of dealing with the forms of power that this new text is rebelling against, this book does the opposite. Since 2011, we have accumulated experience and developed new techniques of resistance that could be considered actions independent from the concept of reaction. Generally speaking, the workings of power have spontaneously generated in a Foucauldian manner several points of protest and resistance. That is to say, "resistance is to be understood as heterogeneous, as a multiplicity of points, nodes and focuses of resistance, not as a radical break at the *one* site of a great Refusal,"[20] but it should also be understood as an unevenly distributed multitude of points, which, in themselves, correspond to the idea of power that is no longer homogenous. Foucault's method "consists of taking the forms of resistance against different forms of power as a starting point"; this analysis of resistance is bound to "bring to light power relations, locate their position, and find out their point of application and the methods used."[21] So, instead of stating and overstating the drawbacks of a subtle, domineering regime, I am going to examine the transversal nature of the new text that resisted the norms.

The Visual

The explosion of graffiti and murals in 2011 will always been seen as a significant phenomenon. Perhaps the walls of Cairo and other Egyptian cities registered the birth of the new aesthetic text and exhibited the concatenation of art and politics. The graffiti text presented all the hitherto unsaid and announced the real meaning of diversity. The form of this text ranged between drawn images and quasi-political manifestos, almost a visual blog. In a later phase, the walls became a contested space between the activists themselves as well as between them and power. In other words, those who were covering the walls with graffiti or stencils or sprayed slogans were drawing their own discourse, reclaiming and politicizing the public space. They were also asserting their "power of presence," in the words of Asef Bayat.[22]

The proliferation of graffiti drawings and murals triggered a huge amount of literature, and I'd go as far as saying it has become over-researched. Because they were threatened with removal and erasure at any moment, the drawings have been heavily documented, analyzed, and commented on. Most of the literature applies the method of practical criticism—that is, read a passage and then produce a close reading. This explains why I am not going to delve, again, into the nitty-gritty of the images or slogans. What concerns us here, is that the term 'street art' has come into being; it is widely acknowledged and taken for granted. Moreover, the mere practice of street art has become a space of conflict between activist artists and power; it has become an expression of the continuous push and pull. For example, painting over the graffiti about martyrs that was drawn on the walls of Mohamed Mahmoud Street in Downtown Cairo in May and again in September 2012 triggered a fiery wave of anger and protest. According to the protesters, painting over the graffiti meant deleting a revolutionary iconic symbol; some went so far as to say that such an act even meant the painting over of history. In all cases, the graffiti itself, as a work of art, became a controversial issue that invited declarations and counter declarations. The scene of the crowds in the street redrawing several graffiti on the walls signified new alliances and endowed the graffiti with a central role that compensated for the absence of discursive practices. At the same time, the act of enunciating political protests and demands on the walls endowed street art with multiple meanings, even if only symbolic. In short, it was a conflict over the ownership of public spaces and an attempt at recruiting alternative spaces.

Much has been said about the graffiti related to and practiced by women. 'Empowerment' and 'agency' have been the two terms used extensively. In her analysis of Cairene graffiti during the first military rule and then the graffiti done during Islamists' rule, Mona Abaza states that "the impertinence in their [the young women's] depictions of the authorities has become one of the most powerful ways of unmaking the system. Indeed, many believe that the military junta had been defeated morally well before Morsi replaced it, thanks to the public ridicule of its violence in popular jokes and graffiti."[23] This is true to a great extent, especially if we take into consideration how the military was unprepared for and shocked by the unprecedented comments that were sprayed all over the walls of Egypt. Part of the shock was that they actually dared to criticize the 'sacred cow' that was the Egyptian military. Many were arrested and charged with inciting violence against the military, especially in the context of graffitiing the military's violations of women's rights and bodies. The very act of drawing and writing on the walls—a form of resistance par excellence—has been taken to mean the emergence of new geographics of identity and a form of agency. It also enriched the research about women's resistance and agency through a minute analysis and reading of all the drawings related to women.

Much of the attention given to the new visual text was due to its novelty on many levels. Discursively, it used a language that had never been used before; it was angry, direct, politically charged, and undisguised. Revolutionarily, it represented a clear-cut expression of collectivity and individuality, and, in this intertwinement, it was a real threat to power. At the same time, it provided a new approach to rethinking the transformation of gender in all its complexity in the dynamics of the Revolution. Most graffiti artists have their own Facebook pages, they talk to the media, and they are involved in the revolutionary act; one can venture to say that most of them are, or, rather, have become, activists at the same time. While most of them were male, several women started to join the field, like Mira Shihadeh, Hanaa al-Degham, Bahia Shehab, and Hend Kheera, who was featured in *Rolling Stone* magazine. All the graffiti drawings were a reflection of the violations committed by the military, then by Islamists, and, recently (although these are very few), by the al-Sisi regime. While violations of women and their bodies occupied a central space in graffiti during the first two years of the Revolution, their subject matter developed, mostly to encompass all violations, mainly of martyrs and prisoners.

The question is, can we really talk about rethinking or reconstructing gender through graffiti? It is a very complicated and a misleading question. With the explosion of street art starting from 2011, many researchers—the present author included—were of the adamant view that the drawings all over the walls of the city pinpointed a radical change in the way gender issues and relations could be understood. This assumption should now be revisited. True, the graffiti drawings, stencils, and writings on the walls came out as a new text that expressed positions hitherto suppressed and silenced. The form itself was completely new and, perhaps, this is the reason it lured an unprecedented level of attention. Yet, after almost four years, revisiting most of the photos of the graffiti drawings related to women and their issues justifies an impertinent question: Is there actually gender in these drawings?

A quick survey of the motifs that are employed in the graffiti related to women could shed light more on the controversial question of whether these drawings were concerned with gender per se or not. Most of the initial drawings were done by individual artists, and, then, some female collectives—like Nazra, Noon Alniswa, and Fuada Watch—contributed to the rise of street art as a tool for enunciating resistance. It is at this point that we started to see more feminist leanings in the drawings. The first batch of drawings was related to the martyrs, so we could see the faces of two female martyrs (of those who have been identified): Sally Zahran (January 2011) and Iman Salama (September 2012). Motherhood also figured in the drawings of the mother of the martyr, such as one calling for justice and threatening *khafi mena ya hukuma* (fear us, government). It was drawn by Kheizer, a young artist who has recently left the country. The next batch was related to the two infamous shameful violations committed by the military: the first was the enforced virginity tests where Samira Ibrahim filed a lawsuit against SCAF, and the second was the beating and stripping of a young woman in public, who came to be known as 'the blue bra girl' and, under a more decent label, *sitt al-banat*. Glorifying both women was a motif that was featured in many drawings (to be detailed in chapter five). One of the highly impactful graffiti scenes showed several blue bras with the caption *la li ta'riyat al-sha'b* (no to stripping the people). The third batch mainly borrowed pharaonic icons and adapted them to the Revolution, as shown in the depiction of Nefertiti wearing a gas mask or the huge mural in Mohamed Mahmoud Street that figured Maat (goddess of justice) leading many women. In some cases, women figured in murals that adapted some Islamic ideas to the Revolution, yet, during 2011, there were not many of that type.

The above-mentioned examples do not acknowledge any specificity of women's position; moreover, they do not address gender issues per se. The positive side of these drawings is that they take for granted that women are equal partners in the Revolution, they are already integrated in the fabric of the street. "The square brought together people who would normally never meet," said Ammar Abu Bakr, a graffiti artist. "People opened their hearts to one another and were no longer afraid of each other. Artists of all disciplines performed in the square, not to show off, but because everyone felt he or she can do whatever they like."[24] One exception could be the batch of drawings related to sexual harassment. In these drawings, outright challenge ("castration awaits you" and "no to harassment" were the most popular slogans) was the main motif, along with the disgust lavished upon the perpetrator of harassment.

When the female collectives came into play, a more feminist approach was adopted. Certain rights were addressed in the stencils that were sprayed by female collectives who launched campaigns for women's rights. Equality of men and women, freedom of dress, combating categorization on the basis of appearance, and the right of women to participate in the public sphere were the main motifs that governed most of those stencils. Some of these were turned into stickers and flags. Perhaps it is this batch that pertained directly to gender issues and women's rights. The importance of these graffiti is ascribable to the way they severed the strong link between women and nationalism. For example, they never portrayed Egypt as a woman (where women are taken to be the markers of identity), as shown in a graffito that was very popular after the eighteen days in 2011. It shows a woman holding up her arm high and the caption says (in English), "Egypt will rise." One of the few blatantly feminist sprayed messages was done by Shehab on 7 June 2013. The sprayed ironic statement says *mokhak 'awra* (your brain is shameful) and was Shehab's way to feminize the Revolution. She explains that this was

> a message to the men who want to silence and intimidate the women
> of Egypt. A message to the men who claim that the voice, the hair,
> the body and the face of a woman is an "awra," a shameful thing that
> should be covered. I sprayed a big brain composed of naked women
> body parts with the message "Mokhak Awra." "Your brain is shame-
> ful and it should be covered."[25]

Does that mean gender was overlooked in most of these new texts? Does the lack of feminist focus justify such a conclusion? It is at this point that we have to pay attention to the new dimensions that have been added to the element of gender. Going beyond gender was a corollary of the revolutionary act. Women protesters were completely equal to their male counterparts from the outset of the Revolution. They both claimed the ownership of public spaces, both were shot and killed, both were arrested and tortured, both combated sexual harassment, and both established their power of presence. However, the most essential common epistemic was (and still is) that women and men, alike, demand social justice. That is why the straightforward monodimensional feminist lens of analysis must be widened so as to include other elements that were vital in the revolutionary context. Adopting the element of gender as the sole tool of analysis while reading the position of women in the new text, that is, the new geographics of identity, does not generate a clear picture of the transformation of gender. The situation necessitates going beyond gender in order to understand how the new visual text disentangles gender from nationalism in the quotidian micropolitics of struggle. These new visual texts are protesting against arbitrary arrests, sexual harassment, physical torture, absence of justice, and unfulfilled citizenship.

The graffiti drawings integrated women in the overall struggle and gave them voice, even if they were not concerned with direct feminist issues. That was not a drawback; on the contrary, this view served women especially in the context of physical violations. All the graffiti related to the virginity tests and the stripping of *sitt al-banat* employed a logic that was completely new to society. In other words, the female body is a human body, and, thus, such violations are not to be categorized as a marker of the woman's honor but, rather, as a proof of the regime's barbarity. The graffiti and stencils, in themselves variations of the new text, shifted women's bodies from the private and silenced to the public and enunciated. Ultimately and by accumulation (and documentation), all this should lead to the formation of new geographics of identity where gender is not the sole lens of reading and interpreting a brave new world.

The new geographics of identity were not mapped by the aid of the gatherings in squares only but also by and through the discursive practices and negotiations carried out by all protesters. The aesthetic articulation of protest displayed novelty and creativity, on both the discursive and strategic levels alike. These drawings on the walls exhibited a high awareness of the political issues and an ability to combine the local and global, not to mention the pride they took in Egyptian history. It is obvious that this generation—the avant-garde—carved its discourse in places that have long been marginalized or neglected, like Cairo slums, cement barriers in downtown Cairo, bridges, metro stations, small towns, and informal districts. At some point, it seemed that the whole country was protesting silently, when, in fact, it was through the new text that popped up everywhere that the revolutionaries declared new positions on several issues, including gender. In other words, these enunciations, even though they were silent, signified the initial mapping of the new geographics of identity where the mapping of boundaries and the dialectical terrains of different positionalities unfolded.[26]

It is understood, then, how this generation moved from what seemed to be a stable position of the gendered subject—promoted by multiple successive powers—to another space characterized by the fluidity of change. The dynamic encounter between self and other allowed for several transversal political coalitions where the barriers between classes were demolished (even if temporarily), as shown in the content of the new visual text. Consequently, such discourse, replete with hybrid discursive interfusions, shocked the traditional bourgeois sense that built its confidence on a stable, whole organic self whose 'language' is proper and 'decent.'

The Eye of the Beholder

It is legitimate, at this point, to ask another question, evaded and deferred for a long time. While most articles on and analyses of street art in Egypt have dealt in detail with the messages conveyed through this form, their subtle political meanings, the histories they resort to, and the creativity that has matured in a short time span, few have broached the issue of reception. Hannah Elansary predicates that the boom of revolutionary graffiti in Egypt "was a sign and act of citizens reclaiming public space from the regime"; it definitely "worked to raise awareness and build community and solidarity among people"; and, most importantly, it "served as a tool by which citizens could (re)claim agency, assert identity, and create their own historical narratives." Yet, she reiterates, these claims serve as a descriptive theory of the whole process; they do not raise the problem of reception or effect. She explains that

> building a better understanding of how Egyptians have interacted with and experienced this form of street art is vital for making claims about Egyptian revolutionary graffiti and will help us test and refine the theories of revolutionary art that are based on accounts given by producers of art.

She fathomed this problem by conducting interviews with fifty-seven people, a nonexhaustive sampling as she has admitted. However, the general responses are diversified and crucial enough to make one rethink the effect of street art. In answer to the question, How do you relate to the graffiti and murals you see?, the majority of the people Elansary interviewed said:

> They did not relate to the images because they themselves were not political in their daily lives. However, many of these participants also made it clear that this did not mean they were against the revolution, or that they did not like street art, but rather that they felt the images expressed only the thoughts of the artists. Again, these responses suggest that claims about community building, agency and solidarity need to be complicated.[27]

Such questions and responses truly complicate the discourse about street art and force one to rethink the taken-for-granted effects. Certainly, the problem of reception already exists, perhaps it has always been there, even in relation to the Revolution itself, yet it is augmented when it comes to the reception of gender issues. Michel de Certeau has explained in his seminal work *The Practice of Everyday Life* that "the presence and circulation of a representation . . . tells us nothing about what it is for its users. We must first analyze its manipulation by users who are not its makers."[28]

One glaring example was the reception of the television series *Sign al-nisa'* (Women's prison) that aired during Ramadan in 2014 and was an adaptation of a play written by the late feminist writer Fathiya al-Asal. The series managed to dramatize the slogan "the personal is political" through a highly sensitive aesthetic camera lens and scored the highest rating in almost all the surveys of the Ramadan series for that year. The main motif of the whole series revolves around what one of the main protagonists, Ghaliya, said: "Prison is not just a high fence and a locked door. Prison can be in a piece of clothing you don't want to wear, people you don't want to see, and a job you hate. Prison is feeling broken and oppressed."[29] The numbers of viewers soared high and the series made quite an impression. Yet, unfortunately, a group of lawyers filed a lawsuit against the minister of culture for having allowed this series, which they claimed "incites vice."[30] While the series was very well received by many, especially those concerned with women's issues and rights, it was deliberately misreceived by the so-called 'guardians' of morality and phoney ethics. Such a reaction is not surprising, especially as it is an eye-opener to the reality of women's daily struggle. That is, the strategy of whitewashing the micropolitics of women's reality, which had been adopted faithfully by the Mubarak regime for the sake of stabilizing a fixed image, has sunk deep into the epistemology of society, or the viewers in this case.

Due to its strength and ability to articulate the unsaid and to go viral, the visual text has been problematic from the outset of the Revolution. Two examples illustrate this point: while the first stirred debates and controversies, the second, although equally controversial, went unnoticed. The first example has to do with Sally Zahran, one of the first martyrs of the Revolution. She is said to have died on the Friday of Rage on 28 January 2011, when she was heading to Tahrir Square and one of the thugs hit her on the head with a club. Her photo appeared everywhere: on pantheons in Tahrir, in newspapers, and in revolutionary paraphernalia. From the very beginning, Zahran's photo showed a young, unveiled woman. Soon the appearance of Zahran became a space of contest, where a veil was superimposed or the photo was blurred. Interestingly enough, Googling Zahran's image results in over nine thousand photos that show both a veiled and unveiled young woman.[31] The multifarious reactions toward Zahran's photo indicate a problem of reception. Walter Armbrust has detailed the "afterlife" of Zahran and found that "martyr images projected into discourse or public space implicitly demanded that anyone viewing them declare a position on what they signified. This is nowhere more clear than in the brief history of Sally Zahran." How this photo has become a space of contest proves the ability of the visual text to unleash all hidden tensions and conflicts. Armbrust explains that

> the central point is that as a means for bringing this wide range of submerged tensions into the open, Sally Zahran was more productive than any other martyr because she highlighted social tensions. She functioned as a prism refracting the light of events; a kind of medium, in other words, that redirects meanings. The Revolution was not about women, but it propelled initiatives to re-think the place of women in society. It was not about religion, but it opened a Pandora's Box of religious problems that the Mubarak regime had deliberately incubated. In the early days of the Revolution, martyrdom was an actively performed rhetorical position—a kind of irresistible force in the eyes of those who took it up as a weapon in their continuing struggle.[32]

One wonders if the contested photo of Zahran had anything to do with the counter revolution as Armbrust assumed in his article. Certainly, forcing a change on Zahran's identity is a counter reaction, yet not for all. As I see it, the crudest reaction came from Sally's family. They published a quasi petition that says, "Please do not publish Sally's photo as unveiled because the martyr was a Muslim."[33] Apparently, clear-cut divisions and extreme polarization started very early, and women's positions were decided according to their appearances. Religion, then, was taken to be a marker of identity, even if the Revolution was neither about religion nor about women.

In the second example, the situation is even more complicated, since it is the protesters (and artists) themselves who have inflicted such clear-cut divisions. While the forced virginity tests, implemented by the military in March 2011, were quite shocking, many hastened to justify this shameful practice. In a great act of resistance, Samira Ibrahim had the courage to file a lawsuit against SCAF. She was attacked and glorified in equal measure. She became an icon for the protesters, a means to challenge and defame the military at that time. Samira Ibrahim received huge support in different forms, yet the most obvious and effective was the visual support. Her name was sprayed everywhere, stencils of her face went viral on the walls, and she featured in several graffiti drawings. One of them showed Ibrahim's face (veiled) on the right and Alia Mahdi (nude) on the left. The latter had uploaded nude photos of herself on her blog in 2011, which caused a huge furor in Egypt and all over the world. In 2013 Mahdi left the country and sought political asylum in Sweden. She has also joined FEMEN, a feminist protest group founded in Ukraine in 2008 that employs nudity as a resistance discourse in some of their protest activities. The graffiti of the two women employed the compare and contrast method in order to defend Ibrahim against the charges that were leveled at her by those who denied the incident of the virginity tests. At the same time, protesters wanted to disassociate themselves completely from Mahdi. Under Ibrahim's image, the caption says, "A salute of appreciation, respect and solidarity to Samira Ibrahim, the daughter of Upper Egypt." A big part of Mahdi's nude body was covered by the following: "Samira Ibrahim: 25 years, was stripped naked by force and enforced to go through a virginity test in full view of army officers and soldiers. She decided to avenge her dignity and filed a lawsuit. No attention, no audience, no media, nobody cares. Alia Mahdi: 30 years, posed nude and revealed her body at her own will. Her photos got about three million viewers, fifty articles, and several talk shows." As problematic as the comparison is, the point of departure of the whole drawing is highly controversial. That is, defending the freedom of Ibrahim meant that Mahdi's freedom had to be vilified and condemned on gender-based grounds. Gender issues were important as much as they served the general political discourse, while any diversion was considered either secondary or retrograde. The overall situation is perplexing. While equality and full citizenship were clearly conveyed in most of the graffiti, with the severing of gender from nationalism, some graffiti drawings revived the traditional (fixed) images, recalling the old notions of gender.

In retrospect, this shallow comparison was totally unnecessary and unjustified, since the axis of difference or similarity is absent. It is a comparison that uses and even co-opts an exceptional incident to declare an ethical position, which in itself opposes the freedom of the gendered subject. The eclectic approach to the practice of freedom and the performance of the body negates the discourse of protest against the violations of the human body. I do not discern any difference between the position toward Mahdi and the discourse of confiscating any work of art, for example. They are both founded on ethical conservative principles in an attempt to appeal to the conservative multitudes. Yet, while doing this, protesters forgot that they were vilifying another woman. It is necessary to problematize the issue of reception in order to avoid the across-the-board conclusions that graffiti empowers women or endows them with agency. It is far more complex than that and will remain so as long as ethical judgments are perennial.

The Iconic

With an Islamic discourse flourishing in 2012 and reaching its peak in June of the same year, women's presence in the public sphere was really threatened. They were not welcomed any more, and, thus, they were condemned on every level: dress, voice, body, and for their presence at protests. Perhaps the climax was when some Islamists declared that even the woman's voice is *'awra* (shameful). It was at this point that many women collectives and NGOs started to come to the fore. Of course, the threat was not born out of a void. The general conservatism that enhanced turning women into markers of identity was already prominent during the Mubarak rule. Kandiyoti conceded that this stance "'normalized' an ethos of social conservatism that now makes the task of ascendant Islamist parties wishing to translate this ethos into codified reality a relatively easier task."[34] It was not surprising then to realize that by 2012, when the military delivered rule to the Islamists, the question was to reform or to revolutionize, put differently: to be or not to be.

Strategically and deliberately, women launched huge campaigns to rescue their hard-won rights. They resorted to commemorating and almost bringing to life all the iconic pioneers who contributed to the formation of women's history, like activists (Huda Shaarawi and Munira Thabet), writers (Malak Hefni Nasef, May Ziyada, and Latifa al-Zayat), actresses (Shadia and Suad Hosni), and singers (mainly Umm Kulthum). The strategy was based on a belief in the necessity of resistance that lies in the power of presence. While the space that was claimed by the visual text was being co-opted, women decided to enter the scene using the same tools that were employed by every political collective. Ashcroft has already taught us that the most effective postcolonial resistance is "entry into the 'scene' of colonization to reveal frictions of cultural difference, to actually make use of aspects of the colonizing culture so as to generate transformative cultural production."[35]

This process of interpolation involves the capacity to interject a wide range of counter discursive tactics into the dominant discourse. To explain, the history of the women's movement was interpolated through employing the iconic text that strived to recolonize space. While the iconic text is a variation on the visual text, it derives its uniqueness from the fact that it deliberately reproduces the photos of precursors of the women's movement, pioneer artists, and activists. The manifestations were multifarious: on flags held in demonstrations, posters, stencils, Facebook profile pictures (and statuses), pins, and stickers. And, since the will to marginalize women was indeed amorphous, women decided to employ the iconic text everywhere, indicating that they were 'against' this will to marginalize them in every place. Women activists and collectives entered the scene; took issue with the street, media, and Islamic and military discourses; engaged with the colonial, imperial, and Islamic initiatives; and never allowed power to push them away to the margin again. By being 'against' everywhere, through the iconic text and by propagating photos of women along with slogans that were turned into necklaces and pins, women achieved what Bayat terms "the power of presence." Bayat developed the idea of presence more and gave it more substance when he says that "the effective power of these practices lies precisely in their *ordinariness*, since as irrepressible actions they encroach incrementally to capture trenches from the power base of patriarchal structure, while erecting springboards to move on."[36] It is a presence that evolved into a contentious challenge, and public space was restored in a different way. By bringing the visual iconic into the public, women managed to subvert, even a little, a discourse that was bent on banishing them from sight and memory.

The New National

Similar to the national anthem, the flag is a national unifying symbol. It is noteworthy that throughout 2011, singing the national anthem served as a strategy to avoid divisions. The same happened with the flag whose co-option went through multiple phases. During the eighteen days, it was waved in every inch of the square. After that, it became a sign of being with the Revolution, it appeared on cars and balconies, and it became an essential commodity.

Interestingly enough, the flag became part of women's daily appearance. In the square and in all the Friday demonstrations, painting the tricolor flag on the face became a cosmetic sign of solidarity. Yet, the public and popular imagination did not stop at that. Away from the square, women replaced their usual head scarves with the flag, used it as a shawl, and wore bracelets of the three colors. The corporeal feminine body 'became' the flag. One wonders about the meaning of that and whether it had any relation to the concept of nationalism. After Roland Barthes,[37] it can be argued that the co-option of the flag reflected the core of the conflict. In his famous reading of a photo that shows a black soldier saluting the French flag, Barthes negotiated several semiotic interpretations. These ranged between the integration of the colonized and loyalty to the nation. Similarly, the flag, in the Egyptian context, signified a symbol of patriotism and citizenship. It functioned as a sign of claiming citizenship and a sign of loyalty. The latter was the most dangerous sign, since every political actor claimed the right to 'sing' the nation as a solo singer and citizen.

Unconsciously, women resorted to integrating the flag (in clothing or as accessories) into their daily lives to reclaim their equality vis-à-vis a majority that was seeking to define the nation in its own terms and set up norms of exclusion, deciding who can exercise freedom, whether discursive or physical. In *Who Sings the Nation-State?*, Judith Butler and Gayatri C. Spivak state that "the problem is not just one of inclusion into an already existing idea of the nation, but one of equality, without which the 'we' is not speakable."[38] Women, therefore, integrated the flag into their daily costume to reiterate the nation, in a way that was not authorized. They were claiming equality, declaring a position, and emphasizing that their presence was part of the national scene. The flag was indeed over-consumed by women, yet it underlined how the female body can function as a message, a position, and a manifesto. However, after Butler and Spivak, this book poses the same questions: "Is it not simply the expression of a new nationalism? Is it a suspect nationalism, or does it actually fracture the 'we' in such a way that no single nationalism could take hold on the basis of that fracture?"[39] What is disturbing here, in the donning of the flag, is that women were consolidating the link between gender and nationalism, simultaneously taking gender away from the real demands. Yet, the novelty of the action here stems from the fact that turning the flag into part of the body is a claim of citizenship. In 2005, when France banned donning the veil in public places, women took to the streets and turned the French flag into a head scarf. Similarly, in Egypt, the female body that was shunned by Islamists resisted through representing itself as a symbol and sign of the national flag that cannot be shunned.

Although several public figures turned the flag into a form of dress, especially in the post–30 June elections where they were filmed dancing in front of the poll stations, Safinaz, the belly dancer, came under attack when she did the same in August 2014. She wore an outfit depicting the colors of the Egyptian flag during a party in a Red Sea resort. A complaint was filed against Safinaz by "angry citizens," accusing her of defaming the Egyptian people and state. The party organizers were also summoned by the prosecutor general. In June 2014, Egypt's then interim president, Adly Mansour, issued a law imposing a jail term of up to one year and a fine with a maximum penalty of LE30,000 ($4,000) for insulting the flag. "Some forms of insulting the flag, as stipulated by the law, include raising, displaying, or trading a flag if it is damaged, faded or not suitable in any other way. It is also prohibited to add any slogans, designs or pictures to the flag," according to Ahram Online.[40] Apparently, Safinaz was not allowed to dance for the nation. Although wearing an outfit that depicts the colors of the flag was hailed and welcomed when the women wearing it danced in front of poll stations, the belly dancing of Safinaz was disdained, since it was done for pleasure, not for the nation. The concept of nationalism, signified by the flag, has become ambivalent enough to include and exclude. While the new national text has been co-opted by all political actors, Safinaz was not allowed by the imaginary we to participate in the process.

It is apparent that all the aforementioned practices stem from the popular, which is besieged by problems of repression. The popular arts are by default beyond the control of any power, and, thus, they tend to subvert the logic propagated by authorities. In Egypt, the popular has become a daily practice that pops up everywhere: in the street, on the walls, in clothes, in music, in songs, and most important in social media. The practice of utter freedom of gender on Facebook and Twitter, for example, not to mention the photos uploaded on Instagram, have been very strong means that resist the rampant and homogenizing discourse of the official media about women, especially women protesters. Several studies have been conducted on the role of citizens in social media, and we can now use the term 'online activism.' Yet, the most important feature is the demolition of old language, the questioning of taken-for-granted concepts about gender roles, and the cruel satire that neither women nor men hesitate to lavish on the Old Guard. One final thing has to be said about the new text: it deconstructs the old language and reveals the political myths upon which the arrière-garde had founded and consolidated their discourse. It is this shocking attribute that endows the new text with power.

3 THE NEW SUBVERSIVE POETIC VOICES

In 2013, Abeer Abd al-Aziz, a poet who has published more than five volumes, launched a project titled *Zat* [self] for Women Poets. The project alerted the attention of the cultural milieu to the fact that there are many women poets whose voices are unheard. To attribute this quasi marginalization to the fact that they are women is a hasty explanation. We should take into consideration the domination of narrative over verse, especially with the advent of the Revolution, a big narrative in itself. Why, then, does this chapter concern itself with poetry rather than the novel or short story? The narratives that were produced by women writers—so far—after the outbreak of the Revolution do not match the expectations of what should have come out of the Revolution. Neither the sensibility nor the language exhibits any subversive discourse in relation to gender. At best, some narratives recall the awakening of feminist consciousness with the outbreak of the 2011 events.[1] Perhaps more time needs to elapse in order for what happened to be rewritten, not only in the square but also in the power relations that shape the gendered self.

Fortunately, the expected wave of subversion has taken place in poetry. Unfortunately, society has forgotten the value of poetry. Consequently, there is no mention of the new poetic discourse whenever gender is discussed. As Dana Gioia writes about American poetry, "to the general reader, discussions about the state of poetry sound like the debating of foreign politics by émigrés in a seedy cafe."[2] It is in the form, language, discourse, sensibility, tone, attitude, and subject matter of the new poetry that we can discuss a new construction of gender in Egypt. However, before celebrating these new poetic voices, we should contextualize them in a long history of verse. Since the 1980s, the voice of women poets has managed to carve its niche in the literary scene. The first generation included Fatima Qandil, followed by Iman Mersal, Safa' Fathy, Hoda Hussein, Ghada Nabil, and Gihan Omar; the middle generation included Zahra Yosry, Nagat Ali, Rana al-Tonsi, Abeer Abd al-Aziz, and Heba Essam; the young generation—whose consciousness came of age with the outbreak of the Revolution—includes Sara Allam, Marwa Abu Daif, Malaka Badr, Sara Abdeen, Azza Hussein, Ghada Khalifa, and Amira al-Adham. Listing names is certainly a tool that lacks accuracy. However, I am simply trying to put names in a broad context. Definitely, there are other names, yet accurate documentation is lacking. Basically, here, I am concerned with the poetic discourse of the young generation.

This generation, mostly in their 20s, with one or two books published, has engaged with the world through the Revolution and its discontents. They are in revolt against Islamists and the military, they voice dissent against a totalitarian regime, they strive to break free from all social shackles, and they are bent on demolishing all fixed concepts that have for a long time shaped the gendered self. They gaze at the world from the lens of women who are besieged by an entangled web of sociopolitical and culture-bound relations. Subverting and challenging these relations, along with the concepts they consolidate, is the main concern of these rising poetic voices. It is at this juncture that poetry distinguishes itself from the novel. As compact and intense as it is, the 'new' poem poses itself as a retaliatory discourse that requestions and upsets the alleged stability. It deglorifies and desacralizes the taken-for-granted worldview, and, most importantly, it does not abide by the main hallmark of modernity, where "at a very deep level, the aesthetic and the social need to be kept, and often are consciously kept, in a state of irreconcilable tension."[3] In their rebellion at the aesthetic and social, the young women poets broaden the scope of gender. Indeed, they go beyond gender and encroach upon a humanist position. Their humanism is in accordance with the definition given by Edward Said:

> Humanism is not a way of consolidating and affirming what 'we' have always known and felt, but rather a means of questioning, upsetting, and reformulating so much of what is presented to us as commodified, packaged, uncontroversial, and uncritically codified certainties, including those contained in the masterpieces herded under the rubric of 'the classics.'[4]

While the poems of this generation spring from the subjective and the quotidian, they expand to the political and social. The convergence of the personal and the political presents an exigent, resistant, and intransigent discourse that reflects the effect of the Revolution as an event that has watered the seeds of consciousness. Although any poem begins from individuation, it, nonetheless, aspires to universality. Whether the aspiration is met or not, it is not guaranteed that it will produce anything that is binding or authentic. Therefore, I am not trying to interpret the sociopolitical struggle by reading the poems; rather, I am reading the struggle from within the poem itself. That is to say, I am attempting to extract the manifestations of the struggle as voiced textually in the poems. One cannot approach the poems with any ready-made assumptions. One should, perhaps, follow what T. Adorno has advocated in his "On Lyric Poetry and Society," where he warns against focusing on the social perspective or the social interests of the works and their authors. His methodology, instead, is to

> discover how the entirety of a society, conceived as an internally contradictory unity, is manifested in the work of art, in what way the work of art remains subject to society and in what way it transcends it. In philosophical terms, the approach must be an immanent one. Social concepts should not be applied to the works from without but rather drawn from an exacting examination from the works themselves.[5]

The importance of highlighting the new poetic discourse of young women poets lies in the key word 'voice.' The binary of silence and voice has always been problematic in feminist theory. While some view silence[6] as a means of resistance, others believe that voice is a medium that should be appropriated by women. Yet, it is all about language, which is not a game that can be easily won. As Teresa de Lauretis writes: "Language, of which we have no mastery, for it is indeed populated with the intentions of others, is finally much more than a game."[7] In this, de Lauretis echoes other feminist critics who focus on the way dominant language limits textual struggle and, simultaneously, provides a means of rupture and subversion. True, we are all housed in language, and poetry is language. Hence, the importance of what these young poets do to the dominant language. They appropriate it to their own benefit and break the social and aesthetic links violently to produce a poem that stands as a rebellious unity on its own. The poetry of these young women is characterized by harsh critique of all the established narratives of society. It is a critique that targets the cultural and sociopolitical norms, enhanced by patriarchal paradigms. Most of the poems may be seen as directly calling into question women's long-held assumptions and related habitual behavior. Revisionary mythmaking is the main strategy employed to carve new spaces for women's agency. Liz Yorke believes that

> the concept of re-vision also carries suggestive possibilities for the construction within culture of an alternative field of identification, inviting a new attitude or exploring a fresh perspective for 'real-life women.' Subjective change might occur most dramatically where the poetic text works to break through culture-wide censorship, silencing and exclusion to bring the reader to a new clarity of vision in relation to its themes.[8]

The main framework of my reading includes two questions. The first is, what are the strategies these poets use to produce an oppositional poetic discourse? And the second question is, how far does the construction of gender in these poems disrupt and subvert the socially stable?

Sara Allam: Kisses and Loneliness

Sara Allam (b. 1989) has published two volumes: *Doun athar li qobla* (Without a trace of a kiss) (2013)[9] and *Tafuku azrar al-wehda* (Unbuttoning loneliness) (2015).[10] Gender relations, as complex as they are in a society that goes by the division of roles, are the main leitmotif on which Allam's poems are based. Simply, she is bent on breaking the rules, in their different variations: emotional, social, body-related, cultural, religious, and aesthetic. The high-pitched rebellious tone of the poetic voice sweeps aside all the stable concepts, leaving no choice for the reader but revision. Allam's decision to speak up and to say the unsaid that has always been inferred from the subtlety of the poetic is really stunning rather than shocking. The chaos Allam causes to all the deeply set conceptualizations echoes Helen Cixous and Catherine Clement's opinion:

> What would happen to logocentrism, to the great philosophical systems, to the order of the world in general if the rock upon which they founded this church should crumble? . . . all the history, all the stories would be there to retell differently; the future would be incalculable; the historic forces would and will change hands and change body—another thought which is yet unthinkable—will transform the functioning of all society.[11]

Indeed, Allam is retelling the whole story differently in an attempt to subvert the rock. She looks back at the roots that are usually taken pride in and propagated as a point of strength. In "Asfal al-matar sawa'" (Equal under the rain), the poet traces back the route to her roots and says:

I am the son of the last pharaoh-king.
My father,
A king who turned farmer after the rain had fallen.
He went to his field
To collect me and disappointments.
My mother,
Daughter of a prince of a neighboring family,
Was setting a kingdom for herself like Bilkis

Before an ominous hoopoe brought her the news of my father's
wedding.
My brothers and sisters,
Crown princes and former princesses.
The eldest
Was left in the palace where he fell for the toilets.
A plumber
Repairing the paths of waste.
The middle one
Hung to my mother and the hoopoe,
Left himself to the birds,
Swapping small chicks with American cigarette butts.
The youngest
Brought up by her lady's maid,
She taught her to cook, do the dishes, and look after children.
And me,
I took after my uncle the ancient Egyptian writer.
I sit crosslegged,
Teaching the deaf to write, but they do not hear.
We are a family without offspring.
The day the Hyksos invaded my people the pharaohs. (*Doun*,
31–32)

Dismantling the original story by transforming, or, rather, claiming,
the historical into the personal and familial is the poet's point of departure.
While all the members of the family abided by their assigned social roles,
only the 'I' of the poem took to writing as a weapon inherited from her
ancestors, yet she is "teaching the deaf to write." Although the image signifies futility and waste of effort, it also implies resistance and perseverance.
By stating that "we are a family without offspring," the poet paves the way
for new and fresh beginnings.

In "al-'Ary hadd al-imtila'" (Nudity to the edge of fullness), the poet
continues breaking all ties and links to the imposed social rules, especially
the concept of the family, in itself the most powerful social and psychological power. She turns the self into a violent self-destructing medium:

I will wrap myself with an American cigarette
Well made,
Light it
And puff in the air.
The room is clad in dark clothes.
I will denude it,
Spit on its clothes
On my father
And the people
And the dust,
Vomit them all,
Turn around,
And take off my pants,
Pee on them
With my frayed organ,
Outworn by lack of use,
Stick my tongue out happily,
And complete my nudity to the edge of fullness. (*Doun*, 19–20)

The violent scene deprives familial ties of their sanctity and indicates that the feminine self is bound to continue her quest for an autonomous psyche, not only by abandoning but also burning. The whole scene seems like a rite of passage, yet it also co-opts a male dominated act: "Take off my pants, / Pee on them." In spite of her assertiveness about her vengeful act, she is a woman who is still overpowered by the dominant "outworn" tradition, the world of male identity.

The quest for agency escalates in "Hadd al-ikhtifa'" (To the edge of disappearance) where the poet declares that

I just came from God's funeral.
He was lying on His white bed,
Eyes closed,
Clean shaven,
Soft skinned,
With sharp features,

Covered in a long dress to the disappearance.
His angels had left Him,
Too busy distributing His estate. (*Doun*, 45)

Allam is taking issue with an overarching truth to deepen the process of revision. The daring statement about the disappearance of God represents her decision to sever all links and commitments to a patriarchal chauvinistic and male-dominated society. This is an utter revolution where all hierarchies are dismantled. The process of reexamining the patterns of self-worth and the power of prevailing symbols is facilitated by the fiery anger and rage. Yet, one must ask: What are the alternatives to this anger?

The answer comes in the title of the second volume *Tafuku azrar al-wehda* (Unbuttoning loneliness). The decision to do without any pretense allows the poet to speak about her loneliness. Yet, writing about loneliness is a painful task that requires incessant trials. In "Aridat azya'" (A fashion model), she admits that "there is always an unwritten poem" (*Tafuku*, 15). Yet, it is also being written. The dialectic between speaking up and silence leads to more attempts at finding alternatives. While the poet has stated that she has witnessed God's funeral in her first volume, she writes in her second volume about her own, albeit small, funeral in "Ganazati al-saghira" (My small funeral). This is the master scene of taking revenge:

All my lovers will stand around,
Holding poems they know were about them.
Only killers know
That a crime leaves a mark that doesn't wash away with death.
A killer takes my book with his right hand,
Pours ink on my picture.
My staring picture like a carved drawing
Is now obscured by ink,
But memory cannot hide it. (*Tafuku*, 21)

In this scene, the poet is inviting the reader to make an evaluative scrutiny of dominant structures of control, to imagine a displacement of the centrality of the masculine. Witnessing her own funeral, the poet turns the feminine self into a mirror that forces male lovers to deal with a sense of guilt and shame. The revenge lies in the trauma of the memory she is leaving behind her.

Meanwhile, loneliness does not solve the dialectic of speaking up and silence. Yet, the fact that Allam carves space for the repressed to come out endows the dialectic with another dimension. "Aktobuhu li ahrab" (I write it to escape) sums up the whole dialectic:

> Poetry also releases pain;
> Reveals silence;
> Lifts the burden of costly confessions off me.
> I write it to escape.
> That's a poem . . . not me.
> I write it for you to see.
> That's my hero . . . not you.
> Poetry knows.
> Poetry tells the fortune of stories and cups of disappointments.
> (*Tafuku*, 13)

I read this as an attempt to construct a place of identification outside the common dialectic of speaking up and silence. The link between poetry and repression, on one hand, and poetry and consciousness, on the other, are recurring patterns throughout the volume. While poetry is the location of pain, it is also the site of subjectivity and agency. As much as it is a medium of expression and confessions, it is also a means of connecting with the inner self. The poem is a double-edged weapon: it represses and reveals. The process of attaining consciousness is loaded with pain. However, there is no other way. One might repeat Audre Lorde's questions:

> What are the words you do not yet have? What do you need to say? What are the tyrannies you swallow day by day and attempt to make your own, until you will sicken and die of them, still in silence?[12]

Allam's funeral is far from being a surrender to death. It is her symbolic image to announce that she is awakening from the dead and starting afresh, free from all ties and links. The poem is her means to redress her lost identity, as a poet and a woman. She reexamines and reenvisions all social myths, constructing along the way her own legend.

Marwa Abu Daif: Mother and Military

Marwa Abu Daif (b. 1980) has published two books, the first, *Zakirat raheel* (Memory of departure), came out in 2008, and the second, *Aqusu ayami wa anthuruha fi-l-hawa'* (I cut my days and scatter them in the air), came out in 2013.[13] While the first book experiments with writing poetic prose, the second came out as a volume of poems and was hailed by critics. Much to my disappointment, they noticed that "what is remarkable about this volume is that most of the poems do not deal with love and the other sex, the main feature of most feminist writings"; the poems, instead, deal with "personal disappointments . . . God and the mother are recurrent figures."[14] Two reservations should be raised on this comment. The first relates to belittling what is alleged to be the subject of feminist writing: love and the other sex. While these are not necessarily the main subjects of feminist writings, there is no reason to belittle them. The second has to do with setting the figures of God and the mother separate from feminist writings. In fact, the 'mother' figure is in the core of feminist thinking and writing, since it allows a wide space for redressing a fragmented identity, whereas centralizing the figure of 'God' facilitates reexamining the dominant male tradition.

Abu Daif's poetic discourse works on several fronts simultaneously. She locates the feminine self in a rigid social tradition, establishes a link between the precarious position of the self and the big narrative of present history, and adopts a role-play of a mother–daughter relationship to communicate her own opinion. While the self in Allam's poems is characterized by her loud and angry rebellious voice, the self in Abu Daif's poems keeps a low profile amid a web of sociopolitical power relations. Although her voice is not staccato, as that of Allam, she manages to reexamine and revise all present suffocating myths with a persevering tone. She poses as a realistic, anguished woman who has found out that the world offers few places for her kind. Out of this realization, she "cuts her days" and "scatters them in the air" of the poem. The metaphor derives its significance from the feeling of renunciation that runs through the volume as a leitmotif.

At the outset of the volume, Abu Daif states her position and explains the nature of her discourse:

> I wanted to say that I sing to the flowers and the rain and the sky, and I write romantically on the aesthetics of passion and bashfulness and chaste coquetry. I wanted to elaborate a poem that tastes like sugar and the colors of butterflies and the waltz of lovers. I really wanted to do so, but what do I do when the sky is toying with a sun that grills butterflies slowly? Let's then sing for a black cat or a street that swallows people or a military waltz for the killed or mass extermination for the benefit of the machine. Let's write on the aesthetics of defeat and the justification of disappointment. (*Aqusu ayami*, 7)

Abu Daif sets the context for her writing, announces her worldview, and faces reality. In this way, she turns the poem into an oppositional discourse and a means for social change. Announcing the subject of her writing is surely not the purpose. Smartly, Abu Daif is establishing a link with the reader through a highly ironic statement that sees beauty in the ugliness. The statement is reminiscent of William Butler Yeats's poem "Easter 1916" where he narrates the massacre of the Irish revolutionaries through the unforgettable refrain: "A terrible beauty is born."

She tries to fit within the social paradigm:

> I rub my eyes to exorcise *efreets*.
> I might be then
> A good decent girl
> Who doesn't offer sweets to squirrels
> Nor kiss the plagued street children (*Aqusu ayami*, 15)

However, she totally fails in "Tamarin al-bint al-mo'ddaba" (Exercises of the good girl). In "Tufaha tushbih qunbila" (An apple that looks like a bomb), she builds her own legend by deconstructing the dominant one. She rereads all romantic stories and almost demolishes them:

> You didn't hear me when I said
> That the woman in white is a ghost,
> Or she might be the angel of death,
> And that Cinderella was in fact limping,
> That is why her shoe fell,
> And it is not true what they said about marriage
> From a prince at the end.
> It was only a severe gangrene from a polluted injury,
> That ended with an amputated leg. (*Aqusu ayami*, 22–23)

Deconstructing the well-established myth paves the way for the self to build her own story. She is reenvisioning all the lies that have always been used and misused by power to render a beautiful reality. Abu Daif's reality is far from that. Indeed, Abu Daif here is voicing the opinion of a whole generation, the one that was defeated and disappointed at the Revolution. This generation, which experienced the Revolution in the square, has realized that:

> Beauty my friend,
> Is not valid for endings.
> Death resembles the world,
> Sudden and ugly.
> Believe me, I, too, collect flowers
> And befriend seagulls
> And I dream to kill time.
> But it is the apple my friend,
> This apple,
> Resembles a bomb,
> And there is a terrible . . . terrible conspiracy
> Inside. (*Aqusu ayami*, 23)

She reiterates her unique position, her different lens, and her awareness of the defeat. She seems like Tiresias, the blind clairvoyant in Greek mythology, who was described by T.S. Eliot in "The Waste Land" as the person who has "seen it all." No escapism here; it is all about admittance and confrontation. The crude confession made in "Bayn bayn" (In between) begins from the personal and escalates to the political and collective:

> I've always been in-between,
> Neither beautiful nor ugly,
> Neither smart nor stupid.
> When I knew dreams,
> They were in-between,
> So was my awakening.
> My heart was pale gray,
> When I chanted revolution,
> My revolution was in-between.
> The oven overflowed for two seconds and calmed down. (*Aqusu ayami*, 28)

From now on, a litany of bitter pain and regret over the ugly (in-between) reality begins. She is truly celebrating the aesthetics of defeat, especially the defeated revolution. It is worth noting here that the poet expresses the power of the Revolution by using an image from the Quran: *The oven overflowed* refers to Noah's ship when it started sailing (11:40). The image signifies and conveys the very strong initial eruption of the Revolution. Yet, it calmed down and everything returned to the state of being in-between. This explains the recurrence of the word "disappointment" throughout the volume. It appears in various manifestations until the climactic moment comes: "Disappointment is not the worst thing" (*Aqusu ayami*, 94). Apparently, there is worse than that. While the poet does not spare a chance to excavate the meaning of disappointment, she insists, ironically, that

> Life is not that bad.
> There is a sun and a sky and a sea and birds and childhood.
> We are only outworn by days
> More than we should be
> And that is all. (*Aqusu ayami*, 95)

This is how Abu Daif cuts her days and scatters them in the air, then she rearranges all the pains and defeats to produce a new aesthetic discourse. She speaks up on behalf of the silenced and defeated. That she breaks the silence over the sense of defeat is a form of resistance to all the fake discourses that govern the political arena. The political defeat has generated a disappointed generation.

While the mother figure recurs in Abu Daif's poetry, there are many poems addressed to the mother directly. Feminists have paid due attention to the mother–daughter relationship; the mother becomes the trusted other in many cases. Adrienne Rich has stated that:

> Mothers and daughters have always exchanged with each other— beyond the verbally transmitted lore of female survival—a knowledge that is subliminal, subversive, preverbal.[15]

The mutuality and equality of this womanly relation seems ideal to construct a new world out of the ashes of the old one, the one that was already defeated. On a different note, the obsession with the mother figure in Abu Daif's poetry, whether as a speaker or an addressee, reveals the poet's desire to return transcendentally to the mother as a place of identification. While Allam traces her roots back to ancient history, Abu Daif traces her roots back to the mother. In "Mama" (Mother), the poet almost cries on the shoulder of her mother:

> We are writing history,
> We document the names of martyrs in the drafts of poems
> That nobody reads.
> We listen to music,
> Memorize military marches.
> At the end, I stay alone,
> I crack jokes nobody understands,
> I contemplate photographs
> Nobody sees except me. (*Aqusu ayami*, 79–80)

In her communication with her mother, the poet gives up any metaphors and decorum. It is the moment of unity and relief from all the pressures, even those of the poem. The quest for the mother, or rather for the sense of unity and wholeness, has paved a route where a new space could be carved, a new utopian discourse, instead of the one smashed by the bitterness of reality. In a role-play, the poet writes "Risala ila abna'i al-sighar" (A letter to my little ones) where she warns the "little ones" that when they grow up they will realize that "the world is very confusing," that they should "beware of Hemingway. You will hate God a lot and you will miss Him more and need Him always," and that is why she begs them not to waste their "energy trying to understand the world" (*Aqusu ayami*, 37). She cuts her days and sews new ones through the mother figure. Yet, Abu Daif's invocation of the maternal ground, the sad confessional tone, and the sense of early defeat all produce a bitter nostalgic feeling to be whole again and to heal the sense of loss: loss of innocence and the Revolution. Only the preverbal link with the mother could help a subversive tone to flourish. The authoritarian power of the military (a recurring word throughout the volume) is subverted by the resort to the mother figure.

Sabrin Mahran: Breaking the Law

Sabrin Mahran (b. 1989) published her first volume in 2014 under the title *Targamat fi hiwariyat al-dama'ir* (Translations of consciences' dialogue).[16] The texts of the volume do not come into a form recognized as poetry; they are a mixture of prose and poetry. Mahran herself has said that she never busied herself with categorizing the texts.[17] Yet, they have been received as poetry. Utter and complete subversion is Mahran's point of departure. She subverts and transgresses the highest patriarchal value, the Word, the scripture, the Law of the Father—a process that generates a long contemplative dialogue with an assumed audience. From the very beginning, Mahran sets her position in two consecutive short epilogues:

If your god had one sin,
It was that he didn't estimate his loneliness;
Thus his agonies were revealed in this miserable world
To join him in his desperation. (*Targamat*, first epilogue)

Quite shocking, the epilogue transmutes the power of God into a state of powerlessness and loneliness—a state very close to a trap where He does not know what to do with His own creation. The politics of presence are changed drastically into politics of absence. On the other hand, the epilogue portrays an ugly world, forsaken by the Divine. Therefore, in the second epilogue, she visualizes the future:

> When I grow up,
> I will be a big disappointment
> For whoever expected
> More than a sudden elopement
> Or a bloody suicide. (*Targamat*, second epilogue)

Apparently, there is more than suicide. Since she has already grown up, we should look for that disappointment. All alone in a miserable world, the poet creates her own dialectic—which might be a disappointment for the reader—by endowing the Divine with the power of watching:

> We must document the scene
> With complete objectivity
> And clear-cut lines;
> Up there, there is somebody
> Who is busying himself with watching;
> He laughs at
> Our belief of his joke. (*Targamat*, 9)

The scene documented in the above poem plays on the dialectic of presence and absence of God. It has become a world full of "hearts burdened with the past" (*Targamat*, 9), toward which the Divine power is indifferent, and in Mahran's translation it is absent. The fact that she mostly uses the pronoun 'we' means she is disrupting the gender binary; she reaches beyond gender. In other words, by negating the presence of God (not in terms of atheism) to take care of this world, she exceeds the limits of the patriarchal feminine and designates a new gender.

To transform the relation between the hierarchies of binary oppositions—subject/object, man/woman, divine/human, presence/absence,
speaking up/silence—is the goal of Mahran's poetics. To achieve her goal,
she initiates a dialogue with Mohamed Abd al-Jabbar al-Niffari. He is
known to be an early Sufi, and his *Kitab al-mawaqif* (Book of standings) is
a collection of visionary poems. The "standings" referred to in the book
has a rather subtle meaning in that each poem or chapter refers to a unique
way in which he is made to stand before God. That is, al-Niffari suggests
that God is present and immanent in the real sphere. His poetry has influ-
enced modern Arabic poetry, especially that of the renowned Syrian poet
Adonis. At the beginning of the dialogue, the poet confronts al-Niffari and
says, "The letter has tightened Abd al-Jabbar . . . tightened" (*Targamat*,
14). This is a reference to his famous saying, "The larger the vision, the
more difficult is expression." Thus, the poet implies that she has seen it
all, or rather documented the scene, to the extent that language cannot
express reality. However, she takes issue with the presence of the Divine,
al-Niffari's belief, by exposing the absurdity of reality:

Now, we are all sitting, me
Bewilderment
The fighter
Divinity
Reconciliation
Crying
Pain, in this forgotten space of the world, staring at each other
comfortably, with inner desires of winning, we drink to our fool-
ishness, because God, in this very moment, is betting on our loss.
(*Targamat*, 24–25)

The defiant scene transmutes the metaphysical paradigm that keeps
humans in a subordinate position. She is disordering meaning and unsettling
significance by placing herself, and all the other emotional constituents, in the
place of equals to the Divine. The metaphoric scene is highly ironic. It is not
waiting for Godot who never comes; on the contrary, it is attempting to over-
power Godot, whose absence is conspicuous and accepted. In this way, she is

"challenging the discipline of the patriarchal word, the patristic organization of value and the social codes organized around the Law of the Father."[18]

Yet, she brings God to the scene again when memory haunts her. It is a burdened memory filled with "the martyrs' blood" (*Targamat*, 116). While she reproaches "the improvisations of memory," and describes her nostalgia as "silly," she turns to God again, who is

> Very far from the scene
> Watching us from there
> Sometimes tells us very short stories
> That might help in fits of crying or sleeplessness. (*Targamat*, 91)

The stories are apparently useless, which explains why she addresses Morpheus, the Greek god of dreams. The stories of reality are painful and unbearable; thus, she angrily asks,

> Oh thou God who is staying on the borders of endlessness /
> Why didn't you give us bigger hearts . . .
> So as to bear all this deformity in what you have created? (*Targamat*, 94)

The rhetorical questions accelerate breaking the Law of the Father and subtly reveal a harsh reality where the self seeks reconciliation and knowledge in the absence of a god. It is the dominant chaos and absurdity (described as a Surrealist painting) that motivates the self to quest for an interpretation of the world:

> How did God start creation unless he didn't suffer from an acute
> desire to speak up
> Or boredom and recurring loneliness
> Or didn't need a mirror to reflect his wholeness? (*Targamat*, 76)

It is actually the poet who is speaking up by shattering the silence over the sacred narrative, the Word, the overarching power of the Divine.

The poet is not denouncing her faith as much as she is announcing her rebellion: "Do not believe anything, do not defend anything, huge

doses of moodiness and absurdity are controlling the world; the absolute .
. . uncertainty and its opposite" (*Targamat*, 115). This precarious position
toward the fixed, the created, the Divine, and the absolute is the poet's
revenge at the Law of the Father that has decreed despair and hopeless-
ness. She has no trust in the Word and implores the others to follow in
her steps:

> Who would believe the truth of the letter after repeated clashes
> with the idea,
> The soul,
> The chest,
> The vocal cords? How would they believe the worn out word after
> that? How could they link Themselves to an illusion of a bigger
> illusion?
> How do they reach a stage of certainty into which they pour their
> hearts and then watch them melting away slowly and euphorically?
> (*Targamat*, 116)

The poet has drawn obsessively on her long-standing suffering from
the Word and the Law of the Father. Throughout the volume, she has
been hysterically exorcising the presence of the highest patriarchal value.
Although she has been voicing collective memories, the process did not
end with restitution. It only ended with a resort to writing: "I will write . . .
I will write now more than I ever did / To avoid this explosion that seduces
my head" (*Targamat*, 124). Having broken the Law of the Father discursively, Mahran has gained one thing, or, rather, she has carved space for
her writing. Breaking the law, subverting the Word, and even the role-play
she plans for God have not rendered her stronger or equal to God. She has
enacted the role of sorceress and hysteric; the latter "unties familiar bonds,
introduces disorder into the well-regulated unfolding of everyday life,
gives rise to magic in ostensible reason," as Cixous and Clement suggest.
Yet, they reiterate, "Both sorceress and hysteric, in their way, mark the end
of a type—how far a split can go."[19] Perhaps the split has stayed till the end,
and, probably, the poet knows that very well since she admits, "We have
been cheated" (*Targamat*, 125). But in opening up the field of subjectivity

to female anger through utter subversion, with its potential for transforming sociopolitical relations between powerful and powerless, oppressor and victim, and killer and martyr, Mahran has managed to reflect the real posttraumatic feeling of her generation.

Sara Abdeen: On the Edge

'Ala hafatayn ma'an (Together on two edges) (2014) is the first volume by Sara Abdeen (b. 1981).[20] Similar to Allam, Abdeen rigorously questions the dominant social ideology and its well-knit discourse toward and about women. Yet, while Allam does so through subverting the masculine tradition, Abdeen revamps women's reproduction of the masculine tradition. As I see it, Abdeen writes a cunning poem where she transforms the unfitting self into the abject. Gradually, the reader realizes that the poetic voice that requestions the whole paradigm is far from abject; it is simply a split self that tries to redress the cracks, and, in the process, all the social hypocrisy is revealed. The paradigm that governs women's life is questioned through an ostensible self-condemnation, belittling the act of writing a poem, and asking God for forgiveness.

In the very first poem, "'Ala hafatayn ma'an" (Together on two edges), the poet announces her position on the margin of everything: "I will stay inside my wild despair and indifference toward the pains of the others" ('Ala hafatayn, 9). Marginalization has led to self-willed isolation or, rather, solitude; it is a location that allows the poet to critique harshly all that surrounds her, including herself. She disappoints the other, who might want to take issue with her that all to be found is no more than "a wasted soul" ('Ala hafatayn, 10). She puts herself on full display, deriving strength from the fact that she has nothing to hide, and, in a defiant tone, challenges the others: "Who would dare to dance with a freak? . . . Who would dare to touch that freak?" ('Ala hafatayn, 10–11). Having described herself as a freak, the poet manages to deepen the chasm between herself and society. Hence, the indifference and ability to critique and accuse.

Contrary to Abu Daif who seeks unity with the mother, Abdeen is affecting more distance with her mother, as a means of denouncing the set of masculine values reproduced and nourished by women:

It is interesting to see every person as your potential killer
I repeat in a loud voice, and my mother says, "Even me?"
Yes, even you. Like all mothers, you want to
Replace me with another whose voice is soft, obedient;
You want me to be satisfied with your fast-cooked food
And to praise it even if I leave the table while I am still hungry.
If you wanted this girl,
You should have picked another husband who is good at foreplay,
And not suffering from quick ejaculation,
And you should have been good at cooking, sewing, and crocheting;
I could, then, have become this satisfied girl who is watching her
mother daily
While she is weaving a web of threads in vain! ('Ala hafatayn, 22–23)

Surprisingly, this piece, characterized by a high-pitched tone of accusation, is titled "Haqa'iq insaniya" (Human facts). The mother is blamed for having accepted the set of values that is propagated by society and reproduced by women. In the last line, she is compared to Penelope, Odysseus's wife in Homer's *Odyssey*, who waited for her husband for twenty years and came up with strategies to put off suitors. Weaving during the day what she alleged to be her wedding dress and, then, unweaving it during the night was one of the main wiles she used. She is taken to be the icon of fidelity. That the mother "should have" opted for other choices signifies utter silence that the poet is shattering by speaking up. Although this act of denouncing the details that constitute women's lives is courageous, we should not forget that the poet has already called herself 'a freak.' The blame leveled at the mother figure signifies not only an attempt at creating a distance from the established social paradigm but also a desire to restore unity, to find a place, to feel whole. The whole poem signifies that this woman is in a conflict; she is in a position where she can experience her multiple desires only in fragmented forms. Luce Irigaray comments that:

The rejection, the exclusion of a female imaginary certainly puts woman in the position of experiencing herself only fragmentarily, in the little-structured margins of a dominant ideology, as waste, or excess, what is left of a mirror invested by the (masculine) "subject" to reflect himself, to copy himself.[21]

In spite of such fragmented subjectivity and conflicting desires, the poet becomes a replica of the mother she blames when she becomes a mother. Interestingly enough, this poem is called "Tamathul" ("Analogy"), where the poet admits: "I am exactly like her . . . a cruel mother" ('*Ala hafatayn*, 95). Yet, she exhibits her rebellion in the act of writing. Aware of her split ego, Abdeen says: "Now, I will write a self-praise poem / It might help me to organize my inner chaos / And to interpret my very surrealist dreams" ('*Ala hafatayn*, 14). Soon, we realize that she is defying her mother:

You know . . . I have a unique spiritual experience
That no one realizes except me, my mother doesn't care for it,
She cares more for organizing clothes on the lines.
I don't care for organizing clothes,
According to her masculine and feminine backgrounds,
Or her petty ideologies. ('*Ala hafatayn*, 14)

She takes her revenge in writing poetry; the poem becomes her place of identification where she can exercise complete freedom: "When I want to write / I can transform any triviality into a poem" ('*Ala hafatayn*, 24). Then, in "Haqiqa ana udrikuha" (The truth I realize), she stigmatizes her writing:

I write trivial poems,
That are not worthy of reading.
They lack organic unity,
Content, rhythm, and rhyme.
But I write, perhaps I might find some fools,
Who would praise my silliness,
Because they can't do more than that. ('*Ala hafatayn*, 34)

It turns out that stigmatizing her poems is another strategy of isolating herself. In the last poem in the volume, "'ndama aktub" ("When I write"), she states that she is "inspired by every ugliness" (*'Ala hafatayn*, 107). Now revenge has reached the brim. If this is the last poem, then all that has preceded it is ugly. The subtlety of designating the quotidian and daily as ugly is the poet's safe exit from the masculine paradigm. In writing, she carves her niche of identity and awareness, as opposed to her mother who is "weaving a web of threads in vain!" (*'Ala hafatayn*, 23). The complex relation of the poet to her mother initiated her search for a whole subjectivity, a position located away from the Law of the Father that her mother reproduces and consolidates. While she starts as a freak, she gradually heals through speaking up about her difference. Paradoxically, it is the desire for being separated from the mother, which is actually a desire for the mother and which has empowered her to confess: "Myself is my only passion" (*'Ala hafatayn*, 62). This self is trying to reconstruct her own space through a new language. Her decision to write the unwritten springs from the fact that she believes language has become so "consumable more than all goods," and, thus, the feeling it conveys is "spiritual isolation" (*'Ala hafatayn*, 108). In other words, the self, that is the only passion, is bound to produce a different language from that of the mother. The reader remains baffled, since the poet has declared her similarity to her mother. Abdeen has, thus, expressed the trap into which her generation is caught. There is an urgent need for a new language that is tied rigidly to the old language. There is a need to rebel against the mother, yet, one cannot attain unity without the mother. One is always on two edges.

"Without Huge Losses"

The importance of these young women's poetry stems from the fact that they provide small and growing pockets of alternative discursive practices. While they have all been disappointed at the Revolution, they did not abandon the dream of change. In their poems, they reject masculine modes of thinking, and they even laugh at them, with apparent bitterness. They refuse patriarchal codes of value and ethical practice. With God being the ultimate patriarchal power, the inscriber of the Law of the Father, the poets centralize him in the poetic discourse either to ask him for explanations, to question him, or to ask for forgiveness. In all cases, they have imbued their poems with a different version of faith, which rejects and subverts the dominant masculine version where women are assigned an inferior position.

Next to God, these poems engage with the mother, either to exhibit an oppositional stance or to seek unity and wholeness. The mother figure brings to the fore another issue that is expressed subtly in the poetic discourse—that of language. How can they reject a whole paradigm while they are using its own language? Can you dismantle the master's house with the master's tools? Apparently, they have managed to effect a certain level of subversion. The language itself is subversive, inspired by the daily and quotidian, and does not hesitate to insert some lingua franca. The images, metaphors, and even the titles of the poems initiate and sustain representations out of which women can change the position of the self and its relation to the dominant social codes. The discursive practice of these poems is actually an extension of the chant in the squares for social justice. If it was not attained in the public sphere, it might very well be attained in the poem's sphere, that is, discourse. This explains why the act of writing is rigorously questioned, assessed, interpreted, laughed at, rethought, announced, and contemplated. Writing becomes a tool of resistance and a means of defiance. Speaking up paves the way for constructing a new place of identification and for providing an alternative position to oppression. The poets do not pose as victims at all; on the contrary, they speak as warriors.

Allam, Abu Daif, Mahran, and Abdeen shout and condemn, question and embarrass, reenvision and rewrite, and speak up and resume a different kind of silence, that of knowledge. Courageously, they admit the painful disappointments (a recurrent word) of thwarted aspirations and the experiences of abuse, loneliness, and rejection. They dare to feel angry to the full and to declare the process of change in a defiant voice that takes different tones. They also shatter the rules of the poem, hinting at shattering the masculine sociosymbolic order. Liz Yorke notices that "revisionary myth-making often attempts to shift the coherences of patriarchal language, not into incoherence but rather into something more, breaking against and exceeding the symbolizations of patriarchal discourse."[22]

Credit has to be given to the first young woman poet who published her volume early in 2011. Malaka Badr (b. 1987), whose volume *Doun kha-sa'ir fadiha* (Without huge losses)[23] was highly acclaimed and celebrated, paved the route to self-knowledge with a subtle confident tone. Through language and intertextual images, Badr willed a journey of self-knowledge and revealed the hidden:

> She seems like a ballet dancer
> With her hands on her head
> And her neck stretched up.
> Another look at the details of the image
> Reveals several pots
> And a sweaty forehead,
> After it has been overcooked
> Without huge losses.
> Simply, she was tidying her scarf
> Under which her hair is crushed
> And cooking. (*Doun khasa'ir*, 38–39)

The huge gap between the outer image and the real (inner) image sums up the reality of women's lives under the Law of the Father. The binary of the ballet dancer and the woman cooking allows the poet to rewrite the repressed and to give freedom to the body that is usually crushed. It is of importance here to note that the title of the poem "Hal kan labud an tudi'i al-nur? (Did you have to turn the lights on?) is reminiscent of Yusuf Idris's short story "Akan labud an tudi'i al-nur ya Lili?" (Did you have to turn the lights on, Lili?). In Idris's story, the hypocrisy of a mosque imam is revealed flaringly as he succumbs to the lure of the beautiful Lili while leading the prayer. Likewise, Badr is revealing the miserable reality of a woman who could be mistakenly taken to be a ballet dancer. The brisk and free body of the dancer contrasts starkly with the crushed body of the woman. The shocking reality of this image is taken by all the young poets as a point of departure toward the search and quest for subjectivity and individuation. They have taken the risk of reenvisioning all the masculine myths and have begun to make their subversive voices heard.

4 MULTIPLE PATRIARCHIES AND ONE BODY

This chapter explores what has been labeled the "gender para-dox," that is to say, the alleged rise of democracy brought along the deterioration of women's rights. Ever since the overthrow of the Mubarak regime, women's rights have been closely tied to the rapid sociopolitical transformations only to discredit the concept of citizenry. Women's rights have always been a slippery terrain where identity is always bartered for some political gains, and, in this deal, the female body becomes the indicator of discrimination, the central point of the argument, and the core aspect of women's positionality. What has made things more complicated is that the web of power relations does not take the form of direct oppression and resistance. Power relations are inherently embedded in the deep state, a rhizomatic structure par excellence. The concept of the rhizome, first coined by Gilles Deleuze and Félix Guattari, describes a root system that spreads out laterally rather than vertically, has no central root, and all roots spread out in a fragmented, discontinuous, and multidirectional way. Any point of a rhizome can be connected to any other point. In Deleuze and Guattari's words, the rhizome "ceaselessly establishes connections between semiotic chains, organizations of power, and circumstances relative to the arts, sciences, and social struggles."[1]

The rhizome, the best representative of the deep state, is linked to the concept of 'multiplicity,' which ceases to have any relation to an origin (the one) as subject or object. It is not a multiplication of a definite concept; "there is no unity to serve as a pivot in the object, or to divide in the subject . . . . A multiplicity has neither subject nor object, only determinations, magnitudes, and dimensions that cannot increase in number without the multiplicity changing in nature."[2] Both concepts are highly useful in understanding the rapid deterioration of women's rights, despite the revolutionary spirit. They both represent the fundamental policy of the Mubarak regime and the trap in which all successive powers were caught. Identity politics that limit women's being to their bodies spring from these strongly woven power relations. There cannot possibly be any reference point, and the origin of such an inherent perception cannot be located. It is woven into a rhizomatic structure. That explains why any sociopolitical discussion of women's agency is always controlled by a twist of essentialism that tends to conflate female subjectivity with sexual differences, in other words, the body.

The eruption of the Revolution—a modern moment philosophically and politically—had among its goals the toppling of the dominant forms of patriarchies. Perhaps, one of the most naïve assumptions of the revolutionaries was that gender relations were to be reenvisioned automatically as a result of demolishing the hegemonic patriarchy, the president. Ironically enough, the fall of the main patriarchy enhanced the more acute conceptions about gender and accelerated the reduction of women's subjectivity and presence into the corporeal body. Having left the utopian and modern moment of 2011 behind, one realizes that all successive powers were no more than multiple faces of a rhizomatic patriarchy that deepened the crisis of the modern moment. Other unexpected factors complicate the scene, and, perhaps, the most difficult one is the role of women themselves in reproducing and consolidating those multiple faces of patriarchy. While they have contributed to the escalating process of extreme polarization, they have internalized the conviction that the body is a means of discipline and punishment that is bound to produce "subjected and practiced bodies, 'docile bodies.'"[3] Amid this complexity, the new revolutionary generation has been trying to rescue the female body from the snares of many contesting discourses. Several patriarchies have contributed to aggravating the situation. Body disciplining, a means of sociopolitical control, became a systematic practice against women protesters and, then, against any woman. While physical abuse and torture of men was interpreted as political, all forms of abuse practiced on women's bodies were taken to be culturally specific and, thus, tolerated.

It is common knowledge that modernism is defined by how an epoch relates itself to the past. That explains why every epoch has its own modern moment, where it views itself as a transition from the old to the new. One can confidently say that 25 January 2011 was one of those modern moments—perhaps the last one—where a new world was born discursively and politically. However, that moment was followed by its own crisis, and one hastens to add that the crisis was a corollary of the modern moment in order to experience the necessary phases of democratization. Yet, the hindrances were multiple as well. In his seminal article "Modernity: An Incomplete Project," Jurgen Habermas explains how neoconservatives have confused cultural modernity with societal modernization. Therefore, they recommend a return to some forms of premodernity or to throw modernity radically overboard.[4] The post–11 February moment was one of crisis where neoconservative and patriarchal ideologies dominated the scene. The creative powers of the revolutionary imagination were removed into the sphere of the archaic; logical reason was marginalized and replaced by a principle only accessible through evocation of specific terms like 'democracy' and 'religion.' The result is that women's powerful presence was perceived as a sin of cultural modernity. The big sit-in of 2011 was a modern moment in relation to gender; it was a utopian experience, after which the crisis took over through the discourse and practice of multiple powers of patriarchy.

A Utopian and Modern Moment

The famous eighteen days in Tahrir Square, from 25 January until 11 February 2011, were proof of the ability of Egyptians not only to acknowledge real diversity but also to accept the presence of the female body in its entirety as both a subject and agent, as a body on the move, as a body on the run, and as an icon of full and equal citizenship. It was so much of a utopian scene, dreamt of for a long time that the national and international media, and citizen media, needed more than two years to get rid of its obsession. The scene managed to transgress all kinds of previously set boundaries between different classes, and rigid identities based on class, gender, age, or religion were reshuffled by the multitudes. It was almost a moment of epiphany where the severe cultural, political, and economic barriers imposed by the ex-regime were transgressed aggressively and easily (and perhaps for one time only). This sweeping will to acceptance that amounted to a synchronized harmonious interaction has lured many scholars and analysts into delineating an almost idealized picture of the Egyptian Revolution. Perhaps that was true, yet it was a fleeting, temporary moment. The two main features were highlighted in Tahrir Square: the interminable welcomed presence of women and the harmonious mingling of Islamists and non-Islamists. Indeed, the scene was very close to a Bakhtinian carnival.[5] The four characteristics that Mikhail Bakhtin has set for a carnival are: familiar and free interaction between people; eccentric behavior; carnivalesque misalliances; and sacrilegious conduct, in the sense of the absence of punishment for hitherto unacceptable behavior. The new cartography of struggle accommodated the four characteristics and, thus, allowed space for a new vision. And that is how the agency of the square formed a collective subjectivity willing to jeopardize its safety for a common cause: a utopian dream. Tahrir Square, then, was turned into a geopolitical location that inflected and mediated any given cultural identity or praxis.

The carnivalesque image of the square revealed that gender is inflected by this geopolitical axis. There are several definitions for geopolitics. The one adopted here is that given by Susan Stanford Friedman, since it leads spontaneously to the position of gender. Friedman is aware that feminists have always insisted that the study of politics is not to be limited to government or state formations. According to her, geopolitics "invokes questions of power as they manifest in relation to space." She reiterates to define space:

> I mean by space in this context not a static or empty essence, but rather the spatial organization of human societies, the cultural meanings and institutions that are historically produced in and through specifically spatial locations.[6]

So, Tahrir Square is not just an area in downtown Cairo but a loca-tion—and Friedman refutes the distinction between place and space[7]—that acquired a certain symbolic political meaning at a definite juncture of history and, thus, is endowed with the ability to stand culturally and polit-ically as a collective subjectivity. Thinking of gender as a constituent of identity in this geopolitical location means "asking how a spatial entity—local, regional, national, transnational—inflects all individual, collective, and cultural identities."[8] For protesters, home was defamiliarized met-aphorically, allegorically, and culturally in the sense that the traditional home was destabilized and relinquished for the new and temporary home represented by the square, originally a space that was culturally and polit-ically constructed. At the same time, whereas Tahrir Square represented a utopian location, all that was located outside it, including its outskirts and entrances, represented a dystopia. Attacks and assaults never stopped, and the feeling of danger lurking outside motivated those inside to over-protect each other. Regionally, the multitudes in Tahrir Square were obsessed with the number of deaths that the city of Suez[9] suffered and the fierce resistance it showed in face of excessive use of force by the police. Nationally, the propagandist media of the regime systematically vilified the protesters and portrayed them as thugs, perverts, and anar-chists who were doing drugs and holding group sex parties. As a reaction to that propaganda, protesters were keen on introducing the opposite image. A Manichean logic thus dominated the image of self and other. On the transnational level, the success of the Tunisian Revolution was a nightmare to the regime, whereas it was the ultimate motivation of Tahrir Square. These were the tenets of the square at that time that configured the identity politics within to combat the deformation without. Where would gender be placed in this geopolitical carnivalesque location?

A personal anecdote might help to answer this question. On 1 February, I was participating in the million-man march in the square. Surprisingly, despite the overcrowding the place was not suffocating, as people were very careful to respect the private space of each other, not to mention the exaggerated apologies one would hear if even a sleeve was ruffled. I became friendly with a woman standing next to me. I cannot deny that it was mere curiosity that pushed me to speak with her; she was covered in black from head to toe (a uniform donned by fundamentalists). She confided in me that her husband refused to join the protest, and, so, she disobeyed him and came on her own, since she "could not stay home and not participate in this miraculous event," in her words. She also said that she had to take a long complicated route to arrive at the square, since most of the roads leading to it were blocked. At the end of our talk, I noticed that the woman's dress was encroaching into the private space of a French journalist squatting on the asphalt, completely immersed in his work. Neither of them minded this metaphorical fusion, and, perhaps, they never even noticed it.

Under the Mubarak regime, similar images were accused of tarnishing the image of Egypt. That is, the juxtaposition heightened the (disapproved of) traditional or fundamental versus the modern, Western, and moderate. The scenography was incredible. In another location, this woman would have never stood in the vicinity of a foreigner, and she would have never talked to me, perhaps, in that friendly way. That her chastity should be protected by complete isolation from the other was not a factor in the equation at all. It goes without saying that such misalliances were repeated daily, where gender was never in the foreground. Different codes of dress and behavior interacted positively (probably that was the only time) and learned a good deal about each other without a single trace of condemnation.[10] Where had the gender gone?

It is not new to say that identity resists fixity. What is new is that the geopolitical location and setting are responsible for a fluid shift in identity. With her husband, the woman acted first as a wife seeking *suhba amina* (safe company). However, his reluctance to participate motivated her to act sacrilegiously, and she pushed gender to the background to bring her political ideology to the foreground. Once in the location, she assumed a discourse of positionality that Friedman calls "situational":

So while the person's identity is the product of multiple subject positions, these axes of identity are not equally foregrounded in every situation. Change the scene, and the most relevant constituents of identity come into play. The other axes of identity do not disappear; they are just not as salient in this particular scene.[11]

At the moment of bonding with the cartography of struggle and feeling part of the collective subjectivity, this woman went beyond gender without abandoning it, and other constituents of her identity were highlighted, like class and ideology.

The significance of space as a situational marker of identity underlined the narrative of Tahrir Square in the eighteen-day sit-in. The overwhelming politics of this locational situation erased the mere possibility of any physical violation, and the female body lost its myth, whereas the female subject restored, or, rather, found, her agency. Hence, the disentanglement of sex and gender. This explains, for example, the complete absence of any incident of sexual assault or harassment during the eighteen days. However, we cannot say that Tahrir Square as a location was degendered, since the very existence of gender as a discursive concept allowed for the situational discourse of positionality. What Teresa de Lauretis viewed in 1986 as a shift in the feminist understanding of female subjectivity was reflected in the dynamics of power and gender relations in Tahrir Square. It was a shift from the reductive view of a woman defined purely and straightforwardly by sexual difference to the "complex notion that the female subject is a site of differences . . . that are not only sexual or only racial, economic, or (sub) cultural, but all of these together, and often enough at odds with one another."[12] In sum, Tahrir Square as a geopolitical location, and a moment of crisis, facilitated going beyond gender and established the female subject as a full agent.

Fragile Bodies

Neither Islamic conservatism, nor misogyny, could be taken as justification for what happened to women's rights post–11 February 2011. The question that has haunted all observers and analysts is: where has the Revolutionary discourse gone after the utopian moment? How has the postcolonial hijacked and co-opted the revolutionary? Any attempt to answer this question necessitates the understanding of the colonial, since there cannot be a post- without a pre-. For many complicated reasons that are rooted in the sociopolitical context, those who took to Tahrir Square in 2011 were of the view that the regime and government then embodied nothing less than colonial rule, in the sense that a small family was colonizing Egypt and denying the people any exercise of their rights. That was expressed implicitly in the discursive practices that resorted to similes and metaphors. Therefore, post–11 February, the discourse in which all societal factions were trapped was that of identity, which is the primary concern of any postcolonial culture. Whose and which identity was to prevail became a façade of a deeply divided society that was not willing to negotiate.

With Mubarak stepping down in 2011, Spivak's famous question came to the fore: "Can the subaltern speak?"[13] Ideally and theoretically speaking, the space was willing to accommodate new politics and to be inhabited by new agents. With colonization gone, the postcolonial subject is now to control his or her own agency. Yet, whose language to speak, which strategies to use, which discourse to prevail, and which ideology to valorize were the contentious problematics that immediately shifted the power relations and gradually weakened the revolutionary discourse and even presence. What is the difference, one is bound to ask, between the revolutionary and the postcolonial? While the revolutionary was bent on starting afresh by rejecting and vacating the ex-colonized territory, the postcolonial decided to inhabit it in a reformative way. Over this contested space, where several discourses were struggling to take control, gender has been unequivocally a defining marker and a subtext.

Recalling a specific example should highlight the difference between the revolutionary and the postcolonial; also, it will explain how women's rights and bodies paid a high price. Since the Parliament elections in 2012 that empowered Islamists, the National Council for Women (NCW) has been in a continuous and tedious process of extremely problematic negotiations with the Parliament. The NCW, founded in 2000 with ex-first lady Suzanne Mubarak as its honorary director, came under harsh criticism after the ousting of Mubarak as a discredited remnant of the Mubarak era. Most feminists and activists were already disappointed at the way the NCW was run, the hefty budgets allocated for conferences, and the ambivalent positions the NCW propagated toward women's rights, especially violence against women. They were aspiring to restructure it and reshuffle the configuration of power within it. Some were calling for doing without it altogether and activating the Law of Non-governmental Organizations instead. The Islamists, on the other side, were of a different view and strategy. On International Women's Day in 2012, a women's conference was organized by the Islamist bloc in the Egyptian Parliament and called for a council for families to replace the existing council for women. The point that the Islamists missed here was the rhizomatic structure of power, the multiple forms of the deep state.

The Islamists' engagement with the existing power structures and their desire to take control over institutions, even if only discursively, contributed to the quick frustration and demise of the revolutionary discourse, and it frayed women's rights even more, turning the female body into an easy target. That is to say, in their attempt to replace women with family and to propagate a specific model of women's agency, Islamists reproduced the very authoritarian power that had forced them, the Islamist bloc, to go underground for several decades. This rhizomatic structure was used skillfully and elusively by the Mubarak regime, as it could accommodate the various subject positions women occupied within that authoritarian discourse. With the Islamists' rise to power, all the conservative social views about women came to the surface. These views have always been there, yet they were controlled by the strong hold of the rhizomatic structure. When the Mubarak regime toppled, these views came to the fore, which accelerated the crisis and demise of women's rights and presence. Hence, the gender, or, rather democratic, paradox.

It Is All about the Body

The experience of women during the transitional phase and later under the rule of Islamists has shown how the body became the marker of identity. To be more accurate, women's subjectivity was reduced to the corporeal body, which was used in turn to augment sexual differences. The power discourse about women—as part of the representation system—has contributed highly to bringing the crisis into the light. It is a discourse that has resorted to the prioritization of sexual differences as a category of positioning and an epistemic perception, and the whole concept of sexual differences has been given increased significance by all parties. In other words, the concept of the symbolic phallus as developed by Jacques Lacan came discursively to the fore of the scene. He defines it as "the signifier intending to designate as a whole the effects of the signified."[14] As the "signified," woman became the other, whose position endows the masculine self with its power. When this discourse took over, scenes of the female body stripped, tortured, or harassed became the norm. It is the justifications of these violations—considered as verifiable experiences in specific locations—that are proof of the inherent conservatism of a society that was (and still is?) reluctant to allow any fostering of women's agency. While the horrific experiences that women went through were propelled by politics, the social web of powers never hesitated to confirm and even bless them. The female body came under the attack of all powers: conservative, bourgeois, Islamist, and military.

The link between experience and identity has had its influence in feminist research, especially with the rise of testimonial literature about sexual harassment. The testimonies in themselves have their theoretical limitations, and, therefore, any adequate theory of experience and identity must explore these limitations (as discussed in chapter five). When experiences are accurately interpreted through the mediating theories and dominant ideologies, they can be reliable sources of knowledge. Experiences of women, then, could provide an understanding of the way identities are closely tied to social structures of power, oppression, and exploitation as well as to the ways revolutionaries organize to resist the dominant structures. The importance of these experiences stems from the fact that they "track genuine features of society, features that possess causal powers, the power to shape the behavior of individuals and groups."[15] The core realist theses about identity can be summarized very simply:

> Social identities can be mired in distorted ideologies, but they can also be the lenses through which we learn to view our world accurately. Our identities are not just imposed on us by society. Often we create positive and meaningful identities that enable us to better understand and negotiate the social world. They enable us to engage with the social world and in the process discover how it really works. They also make it possible for us to change the world and ourselves in valuable ways.[16]

The experiences of women, documented in every possible way, show that there is no way out of representation. Resistance to politically incorrect representations resorted to the strategy of speaking the truth in the face of power and voicing all violations not from an approach of victimization. Reinscribing and reinstating the female body in the public sphere was a defiant strategy, in spite of all the risk it entailed; that at least managed to circumscribe the discourse of the symbolic phallus and could keep the concept of presence alive. Presence and visibility of women were meant to be abolished very early with the incident of the virginity tests,[17] of which the underlying message was that the female body is to be tested, examined, controlled, and humiliated.

Islamic Bodies

The moment Morsi was declared president, his supporters took to the streets to celebrate. Part of this celebration entailed verbally harassing any unveiled woman by shouting "your kind is to disappear soon."[18] That was alarming and frightening. Yet, that such an aggressive attitude came out verbally was a positive sign, as if allowing all the past repression to evaporate into words. For a while, unveiled and veiled women suffered on the streets from men and women stopping them to lecture about the proper Islamic dress. With veiled women especially being harassed, the honeymoon with Islamists was over. Because this was daily, common, personal, and, perhaps, cultural, no power could care less. After all, it is always the woman's fault. And this is where the personal and the political became intertwined.

The media discourse and propaganda about the rise of Islam did not eliminate the incidents of sexual harassment. Sexual harassment had been plaguing Egypt since before the Revolution and was used extensively by the counterrevolution, to the extent that a march demanding an end to this form of violence was attacked. Towards the end of 2012, a mob of hundreds of men assaulted the women participating in this march, with the attackers overwhelming the male guardians and groping and molesting several of the female marchers in Cairo's Tahrir Square. When some parliament members asked for legislation that criminalizes sexual harassment, Azza al-Garf, a female parliament member and a member of the

Muslim Brotherhood (MB), strongly slammed the suggestion, when she said in 2012 that to pass such legislation was "not done" (meaning that it was not acceptable) and it is the woman's responsibility since what she wears triggers harassment.[19] In addition to being an almost obsolete rhetoric, what al-Garf said brings the whole discourse back to square one. All powers were bent on forgetting the fact that the Revolution started as a protest against the incessant acts of physical torture and humiliation. What started as an attempt at restoring dignity to the human body ended up as a complete condemnation of the body that does not match a specific ideology. It is not surprising, then, that one of the very early efforts of the Islamists was to organize medical convoys to villages to circumcise girls. Even if only discursive, this position is very close to what the Military Council did to the arrested women: virginity tests.

The fiercest confrontations in the arena of identity politics occurred under the cover of protecting identity. The fifty-seventh session of the Commission on the Status of Women (CSW) at the United Nations (UN) headquarters (4–15 March 2013) ended with agreed conclusions to stop all forms of violence against women. On 14 March 2013, the MB in Egypt issued a statement condemning the CSW's draft declaration, saying that in it were "articles that contradict established principles of Islam, undermine Islamic ethics and destroy the family . . . [and] would lead to complete disintegration of society, and would certainly be the final step in the intellectual and cultural invasion of Muslim countries."[20] The hyperbolic language—"complete disintegration" and "final step"—is meant to lobby a society that is already conservative and is suspicious about international conventions that were signed and ratified during past eras. The reproduction of all previous authoritarian discourses was shocking, yet it was neither functional nor justified. The way Hoda Elsadda engaged with the issue is very telling:

> "Saving Muslim women" has been a battle cry since colonial times, and more recently during the military operations in Afghanistan and Iraq, and has been manipulated to justify invasions. Conversely, the cultural specificity argument of "our women are different" as well as "we must protect our values" has also been

the battle cry of authoritarian Muslim regimes to justify human rights violations and the suppression of rights. The rhetoric is painfully familiar and the aim continues to be the same: using scare tactics to silence your opponents and divert attention from the real issues at stake.[21]

Resorting to the identity discourse did not initiate the expected incitement and lobbying. The strategy of claiming that ending violence is a tarnish on women's Islamic identity triggered another fierce debate between the remnants of the Mubarak era—who had never previously bothered about women's rights—and Islamists who were busy occupying the whole space, discursively, institutionally, and physically. Meanwhile, gender remained a subtext that reignited the revolutionary discourse and led to the creation of a novel discourse about women. While it cannot be said that the paradoxical situation empowered women, it definitely revealed the frayed discourse of power.

Sadly enough, between the two poles that were in conflict over power—defined as Islamists and the old regime—women were busy defending their bodies from harassment and vilification. To make things worse, their marches and protests were systematically assaulted, as mentioned above. The gap between discourse as a shield and action as activism was populated with women who resorted to controlling their representation and putting off the silence that had been imposed on their voice. Women, hitherto used and abused, made their presence visible, through their testimonies about sexual harassment. Bill Ashcroft has deftly stated that "the scandal of *testimonio* for post-structuralist theory in particular is its shameless construction of presence, through the invocation of the speaking voice, and the syntax of conversation."[22] It seems paradoxical that Ashcroft categorizes the voice of testifiers as a postcolonial strategy, that of interpolation, while, in reality and in the Egyptian context, it was quite shocking. Put differently, shifting the practices against the female body from the private and dark to the public and political was a breakthrough.

At the peak of resistance, all the political parties were lobbying against Islamists with a discourse that placed gender in the center (our women and their women), and power relations came into fierce play through a gender cloak: both camps claimed that they were bent on protecting women's identity, which goes hand in hand with the country's identity. At this point, it was clear that women, their image and position, were taken to be the marker of the cultural identity of the nation. Anne McClintock explains the process:

> Excluded from direct action as national citizens, women are sub-sumed symbolically into the national body politic as its boundary and metaphoric limit . . . . Women are typically constructed as the symbolic bearers of the nation but are denied any direct rela-tion to national agency.[23]

Because women were taken to be the transmitters and producers of the national cultural identity, they were denied agency by being forced politically and discursively to conform to a gendered discourse that overlooked all sociopolitical and cultural differences. Agency does not mean the freedom to act, but, rather, "the assumption of human sub-jectivities that create meanings and act in negotiation with the systemic conditions of the social order, however circumscribed."[24] As the iconic representation of culture and a marker of national boundaries, women under the rule of the Islamists continued to experience several forms of physical, discursive, and symbolic violence, based on the denial of agency. Thus, sex and gender were rendered indistinct, and the female body became the target. Moreover, the use of women in the process of escalating political polarization aggravated the situation. No politi-cal discourse or practice was exempt from that charge. Unfortunately, women contributed to the process of polarization, where, again, their presence was visible and conspicuous.

Why Do They Hate Us?

With women being liable to physical and discursive attack, one cannot but ask: why do they hate us? The question opens Pandora's box. Is it simple misogyny or institutional vision? Both, perhaps, feed the hostility toward women in the public sphere. In May 2012, *Foreign Policy* magazine devoted the issue to sex (another problematic theme). In that issue, Mona Eltahawy, a freelance Egyptian–American journalist, wrote an article titled "Why Do They Hate Us?"[25] (after the famous American motto) in reference to Arab men. The context is important. In November 2011, Egyptian police beat Eltahawy, breaking her left arm and right hand, and sexually assaulted her. She was detained by the Interior Ministry and military intelligence for twelve hours. Alongside Eltahawy, several young people died, and hundreds were arrested. Yet, Eltahawy had the luxury of going on air immediately after her release, and she testified to what had happened to her. The solidarity she received from the revolutionary protesters was immense, not to mention the praise she got for her stamina and courage. Her testimony was circulated widely as proof of the brutality of the military junta.

When Eltahawy wrote this piece, she gave it the subtitle "The Real War on Women Is in the Middle East." She smartly listed all kinds of violations women suffer from in the Arab World. So, Egypt, Yemen, Saudi Arabia, Libya, and Tunisia were thrown in the same basket. Between female genital mutilation and being banned from driving, Eltahawy left nothing out. At the end, she asked, "What is to be done?" and replied saying:

> First we stop pretending. Call out the hate for what it is. Resist cultural relativism and know that even in countries undergoing revolutions and uprisings, women will remain the cheapest bargaining chips. You—the outside world—will be told that it's our "culture" and "religion" to do X, Y, or Z to women. Understand that whoever deemed it as such was never a woman. The Arab uprisings may have been sparked by an Arab man—Mohamed Bouazizi, the Tunisian street vendor who set himself on fire in desperation—but they will be finished by Arab women.

Not surprisingly, the article received more than three thousand comments on *Foreign Policy*'s site. Instead of analyzing the reasons behind such violation, Eltahawy replicates and reproduces the approach of the Eurocentric feminist methodologies that extract sex from the whole context, only to render women's struggles ahistorical. To lock the whole struggle into the body is to deny women any agency, even if the other powers are doing just that. Moreover, she laments the position of women in complete disregard of the kaleidoscopic knowledge of the Egyptian political scene she gained as an eyewitness. That she is both an outsider and insider is a rich asset Eltahawy squandered. She could have made the operations of discursive power visible to draw attention to what is left out of feminist theorizing, namely, "the material complexity, reality, and agency of Third World women's bodies and lives."[26]

Eltahawy's piece invited several reactions:[27] some banish her argument, some were on the defense, and some critique the analytical framework. The main concern here is the latter, and it is best expressed by Gigi Ibrahim's post on her blog. As a member of the Revolutionary Socialist Organization, Ibrahim is totally against attributing the violations against women to an inherent gendered hatred. She explains:

> Women in the Middle East are not oppressed by men out of male dominance, they are oppressed by regimes (who happened to be men in power) and systems of exploitation (which exploit based on class not gender). Having women in power in a flawed system will not "fix" the problem either. We had a women's quota in Mubarak's parliament, did that change anything for women in reality? It was all ink on paper. Even after revolution, women are consistently used for political grounds by crony political parties. Explaining why women are oppressed without touching on any of the historical, political, or economical aspects of Arab countries, which are not all the same as she tends to generalize in her article, couldn't be more delusional than this piece.[28]

Ibrahim's argument calls for a different approach that merges women's lives and struggles into the historical, political, and economic aspects of society. Put differently, women's lives are contextualized into the rhizomatic structure. Furthermore, one cannot but notice the focus on class, an essential factor that explains the politics of domination and exploitation. The Marxist tone of Ibrahim's argument is not new in the field of feminism, and it has been revived recently in many parts of the Third World. The argument becomes all the more valid since it offers a realistic explanation of the position of women in post-Revolutionary Egypt. A close look at the program launched by Islamists (whether that of the party or presidential campaign) proves that neoliberalism is to be revived, and it is women, as has always been the case in the Third World, who are bound to dearly pay the price. Therefore, sexual difference as the sole factor of analysis does not mirror reality, whereas the factor of class, in addition to the sociopolitical factors, establishes a firm link between activism and academia. Similarly, patriarchy as the base of interpretation does not mirror reality, whereas the factor of power relations guarantees women's struggle to be fruitful, not debilitating. In spite of the international fame Eltahawy's article received, most of the local reactions the article triggered aimed at revealing the falsity of the essential subjugation of women and locating it instead in history; some went further and linked it to the modes of production as Ibrahim did. Yet, the question is still valid: Is it misogyny?

It is highly misleading to blame patriarchy across the board, since this yields a simplistic interpretation that renders a nebulous understanding of the power dynamics. As a mere abstract concept, patriarchy does not provide a space for responsibility or accountability. It is unrealistic to treat patriarchy as a coherent project that stands on its own, devoid of any other factors. Prominent Turkish scholar Deniz Kandiyoti has written three successive articles since 2011 about the trajectory of women's rights in the Arab Spring. In March 2011, she launched the series with "Promise and Peril";[29] it was followed in June 2012 by "Disquiet and Despair";[30] and the last one came out in January 2013 under the title of "Fear and Fury."[31] According to her, the promise of 2011 has rapidly faded, only to give its place to peril and despair. The comparative lens through which Kandiyoti reads the situation renders a complete panoramic picture that spots the complexities of women's rights in the scene of revolt. The key questions and problematics raised by Kandiyoti form the backbone of the situation. Kandiyoti's reading of the crisis takes into consideration the multiple powers in play, and, so, breaching women's rights is a result, not a corollary; in other words, violating women's rights is the necessary manifestation of the dynamics of power. In "Fear and Fury," she argues that misogyny is not the politically correct interpretation of the violation of women's rights and bodies. She believes that, in order to understand the multiple faces of patriarchy, we must

> turn our attention to the holders of political power and ask how, when and why they choose to become accessories to misogynistic atrocities and/or collude with individuals, groups or movements that perpetrate them. That is why people are on the streets. Their target is no longer just women and their bodies but the body politic itself.[32]

Not only are the state and power relations, which is the rhizomatic structure, implicated in most acts of violence against women, but they are also in any truncation of the democratic path in general, of which women's rights are part and parcel. But most important is that the authority, be it the police or military or Islamists, never *decided* to collude with the perpetrators of such violence. On the contrary, sometimes authority was directly complicit in the violations for political reasons. Throughout all these atrocities, the perpetrating and complicit powers have employed the social conviction that patriarchy exists to their own interest and benefit.

While we cannot deny the existence of patriarchy, we cannot deal with it as the classical orthodox patriarchy that has been dominant for decades, where direct subjugation of women was the normative practice. What we face now is a new form of patriarchy, most active in the political arena, where usurping and asserting power is the compass that designates how gender is to be perceived. In an optimistic tone, Kandiyoti states that what we witness now marks the fading power of classical patriarchy, yet it is

> a new phenomenon I call masculinist restoration [that] comes into play at the point when patriarchy-as-usual is no longer fully secure, and requires higher levels of coercion and the deployment of more varied ideological state apparatuses to ensure its reproduction. The recourse to violence (or the condoning of

violence) points not to the routine functioning of patriarchy or the resurgence of traditionalism, but to its threatened demise at a point when notions of female subordination are no longer securely hegemonic.[33]

Obviously, patriarchy has pulled itself together and come back through the various political powers that were bent on silencing or even hijacking the Revolution. Because this form of the neo-patriarchy is not directed toward women only, one has to make sure that all power relations are taken into consideration. However, women might suffer more, because the legitimacy needed to protect and strengthen women's rights is absent, and, if existing, it is definitely fragile. The ambivalent perilous record over women's rights since March 2011 broke the promises of and wasted the aspirations for inclusive democracy. The loss of the utopian space, carved during the famous eighteen days, might seem less catastrophic if we contend that women's rights and agenda never achieved the necessary legitimacy at the popular level (in spite of the conspicuous presence of women and feminist NGOs). Since 2011, women's rights have been relegated to a secondary position where the discourse of face value nationalism took over (interchangeably with chauvinism, especially after 30 June), bringing down the complex grid of issues into a revolution and a counterrevolution, and, recently, all forms of struggle were sacrificed for the sake of Egypt's 'war on terrorism.' In this crude political conflict, women have been repeatedly used as ideological markers. However, I hasten to add that the multiple means by which women have been used by the political parties, the media, and all authoritarian entities are not new.

It is at this point that one must pose the Foucauldian question about resistance. He has stated that "where there is power, there is resistance, and yet, or rather, consequently, this resistance is never in a position of exteriority in relation to power."[34] Any power generates its resistance; it is born with its resistance. True, women have been resisting from the beginning, yet the signs of resistance are what should be reconfigured by changing the lens of analysis. The term 'women's movement' has always been constantly used by activists and tirelessly employed by analysts. Likewise, Western constituencies have always referred to a vague 'women's movement' in Egypt—a term that brings to mind the agenda set by state feminism that managed to rally (and sometimes integrate) a big part of the civil society. Apart from that, there have always been some women's NGOs whose discourse runs against the grain of the mainstream. Generally speaking, the alleged 'women's movement' was surely hijacked by the modern state and the rhizomatic structure for their own good. Therefore, the Western model of a solid movement with a clear-cut agenda is not valid in Egypt. The constraints of the various authoritarian rules would never allow a women's movement to flourish in the sociopolitical scene. Also, the adherence of the state to all the modern UN demands—like education, job employment, wage equality, or posts in public office— was the legitimate means of hijacking and even co-opting any women's movement. This is also one of the reasons that make referring to a solid patriarchy difficult, as explained earlier. Yet, since women in Egypt have always had a powerful presence, which came to its highest point with the rise of protests in 2011, one should think outside the box of Western models of movements.

Women's presence in the Revolution and its aftermath has been so conspicuous that it could not pass unnoticed. Without the formation of a movement per se, the incessant presence of women in the public sphere and the media led to the creation of another space, not as utopian as the previous one; it is a space of resistance filled with revolutionary consciousness. Paradoxically, it was the ugly abuses and the realization that all governments were bent on curbing women's rights that set the point of departure for the process of self-consciousness. As early as 1986, de Lauretis contended that the history of revolutionary movements has shown that consciousness is not the result but the process, where consciousness of self, including feminist and class consciousness, "is a particular configuration of subjectivity, or subjective limits, produced at the intersection of meaning and experience."[35] Having experienced taking to the streets, women strengthened their own position and developed their own forms of resistance through the form of "collective action by non collective actors."[36] Women made their presence highly visible through resorting to ordinary activities and the practices of everyday life. It is in the daily micropolitics and extreme ordinariness that women were capable of asserting their vision by bringing the personal into the political. In other words, women could restore their lost space albeit in a different form; they managed to consolidate this space discursively and physically. Now, with the liminal moment gone and a new semblance of hierarchy taking shape, it is a priority to achieve legitimacy of women's rights on the popular level. How to penetrate the rhizomatic structure and imbue it with a feminist discourse is quite a challenge.

5 THE POLITICS OF MEMORY

I n 1995, I enjoyed the privilege of attending the fourth UN World Conference on Women, held in Beijing, China. Stamped on my mind are two things: the group of stunning women I met and the World Public Hearing on Crimes against Women.[1] Those testifying recounted and recalled their worst memories: war violence, ethnic violence, fundamentalist violence, circumcision, migration, female infanticide, and trafficking. These women came from all over the world to prove the essentiality of memory. The program of the event was printed on papyrus paper, and had the Egyptian goddess of justice, Maat, featured on the front page. The vision and position of the event organizers showed their awareness of the importance of memory amid power relations. They expressed their vision through this statement written into the program:

> We need to listen to the voices of those who do not share that power; to see these violations through the eyes of the powerless, of those who are on the edges . . . knowing that from the peripheries of power, the world is seen differently; knowing that from the margins comes a new sense of hope, another way of being. And the public hearing seeks to be a voice from the peripheries of this power, for it seeks to speak of this great violence. It comes

from an overwhelming silence; a silence that speaks . . . of retrieving memory from forgetting.

The recollected stories of the women testifying were intended to give voice to the voiceless and power to the powerless. That the world is seen differently from the peripheries is true, but it is also true that the world is always seen differently through the eyes of women. In the context of the public hearing, the margins were empowered, and fixed power relations were subverted by the demand for accountability. Put differently, the master story was subverted by giving voice to *her*-story. The analytical challenges that memory poses cannot be addressed successfully through a linear, coherent, and univocal itinerary. Some theoretical approaches aim to develop analytical frameworks, while others engage in more concrete perspectives that cut across studies of memory: historical, political, individual, and social. I hope that these multiple approaches can converge and shed light on the very elusive subject of the sociopolitical construction of memories and meanings of the past, or, rather, the near past. How Egyptian women have used memory post–11 February 2011 as a shield against repression and how they turned memory into a tool of resistance are the two issues that I am to investigate here.

The Rise of Memory

It was in the 1990s that the politics of memory, of remembering and of forgetting, gained momentum in Egypt. The efforts to combat marginalization of women in all disciplines resulted in a surge of interest in the retrieval and inclusion of women's work, stories, and artifacts. At the same time, giving voice to the voiceless—mainly poor and powerless women—formed the backbone of research projects launched by Egyptian NGOs. In academic circles, women's autobiographies and memoirs, along with other forms of writing, became the primary sources of many dissertations. In the literary arena, women writers were encouraged to write testimonies about their writing career, with a focus on the difficult position of being a woman writer. Those engaged in the field of literary criticism will never forget that rescuing the name of Alifa Rif'at[2] from oblivion was a major breakthrough.

In retrospect, it is apparent that memory was gaining momentum. This is because the interest in memory was still young in the world. Actually, the efforts to theorize memory from the perspective of feminism in the United States, for example, started in the 1980s. Marianne Hirsch and Valerie Smith note that

> the first attempts occurred at a 1986 conference at the University of Michigan, published as a special issue of the *Michigan Quarterly Review* on "Women and Memory" and edited by Margaret Lourie, Domna Stanton, and Martha Vicinus in 1987. These editors and authors use the concept of "memory" to define the field of women's studies as a form of "countermemory" and feminist scholarship, literature, and art as a means of redressing the official "forgetting" of women's histories.[3]

In Egypt as well, the efforts of activists and feminists were heading toward forming a countermemory or, rather, subverting the master narrative in which women have been completely marginalized at worst and sidelined at best. With the turn of the new millennium, it was common to come across projects that worked on recovering women from the past and exposing the processes by which they were made absent. The main point of departure for such projects was located in the discipline of history studies and, then, proliferated in the social sciences and humanities generally. Many prominent researchers started rewriting history from a gender approach that integrates women into the archives, with the purpose of changing the dominant discourse.[4] Within this context, the Women and Memory Forum (WMF) was founded in 1995.[5] Producing alternative knowledge has been the aim of the WMF from the very beginning "in order to reshape power relations within the different social structures in such a way that would support and maintain human dignity in the face of all forms of discrimination."[6] The WMF has fostered a wide range of interest in theorizing memory from the perspective of gender; this interest includes academic research in Islamic and modern history, rereading archives, republishing autobiographies, researching oral history, and rewriting folkloric tales, performances, and translations. These early efforts managed to sensitize readers, spectators, and sometimes institutions to gender issues.

However, that was not an easy task. Both the intelligentsia's and the state's reaction was either hostile or indifferent. While the former has always trivialized the feminist approach, state feminism was not about to tolerate any revival of memory or reconstruction of the collective memory outside its power zone. Naturally, countermemory was partially co-opted by the state. Since state feminism consolidated the link between the woman question and nationalism, the revived memory was meant to serve the same purpose. Denying diversity and dealing with women as the cultural markers of the nation, the state represented itself as the main scribe of official (correct) history that should not be tarnished by other stories, including, of course, *her*-story. One could venture to say that there was an undeclared conflict between the official story, propagated by the maximum power of the state and the other sidelined story—or a conflict between official registered memory and collective spontaneous and deliberate memory. Whatever it was, there is no doubt that what have been and still are acknowledged as locations of memory (*"lieux de mémoire"*)[7] are highly contested. For example, while the state version has always started from the role of women in the 1919 Revolution, historians and researchers would go back further than that to highlight the influence of the French campaign in 1798 on the identity politics of gender in Egypt. That is to say, while the state has always singled out individual women from recent history and turned them into icons for its own benefit, researchers have tended to reread history so as to integrate colonization and class as two essential factors that contributed to the formation of gender politics from the beginning of the nineteenth century onward.

These locations of memory, created and celebrated by the state apparatus, became the markers of official history. Pierre Nora, the French historian, explains that these locations of memory "originate with the sense that there is no spontaneous memory, that we must deliberately create archives, maintain anniversaries, organize celebrations, pronounce eulogies, and notarize bills because such activities no longer occur naturally." In other words, "without commemorative vigilance, history would soon sweep them away." Commemorating such memories becomes an act of defending and fixing, of identity. The problem is that power selects what to commemorate and glorify. In this eclectic approach, conflict ensues. The result is that these locations of memory become "moments of history torn away from the movement of history, then returned; no longer quite life, not yet death, like shells on the shore when the sea of living memory has receded."[8] Tearing certain figures and events from history for the sake of creating a linear developmental story about women has been the policy of the state.

The collective memory, the one that is acted out spontaneously by a group, revived by women groups and feminist researchers, differed from those locations of memory created by the state and from the historical records promoted by official historians, in other words, those acknowledged by the state. These official records are reflected in school books, the annual celebration of International Women's Day, state-run media, and all other apparatus that promote the image of the nation. Collective memory is different in form and content. Maurice Halbwachs defines collective memory as "a current of continuous thought whose continuity is not at all artificial, for it retains from the past only what still lives or is capable of living in the consciousness of the groups keeping the memory alive. By definition, it does not exceed the boundaries of that group." History, and I would add locations of memory, "gives the impression that everything—the interplay of interests, general orientations, modes of studying men and events, traditions, and perspectives on the future—is transformed from one period to another."[9] A quick skim of current history textbooks reveals that systematic, smooth periodization is the official approach to perceiving history. The story of women, as advanced and promoted by the state, has always been glamorous due to the unity and linearity of the approach. Textbooks, television propaganda, and newspaper stories have always dealt with women's history as moving from one point to the other in an accumulative process, with the ultimate success assigned to the current power. From the point of view of official history, the story of women has always revolved around the basic universal modern rights: suffrage rights, the right to work and have an education, and the right to health.

Surely, the story of women, like any other story, entails diversities and discrepancies. Yet, the woman whose image was highly celebrated by the state apparatus emanated from one perception: the woman whose agency is always mediated through men, that is to say, she either sacrifices for her son or husband or for her country. For example, Huda Shaarawi, one of the leaders of the feminist movement in Egypt in the early twentieth century, is always introduced as the woman who challenged British officers when Egypt was under British occupation, without any mention of the power she derived from being a descendent of the aristocratic class. There is, moreover, no mention of the first women martyrs during the 1919 Revolution. On 16 March 1919, three hundred Egyptian women took to the streets demonstrating against British occupation. On that day, Egypt acquired its first woman martyr of the anticolonial struggle: Hamida Khalil (Umm Saber), who was shot down in front of the Hussein Mosque in a confrontation between the demonstrators and the police. Egyptian women who marched in celebration of their political rights in 1956 carried posters of Huda Shaarawi and Hamida Khalil.[10] Later on, the name of Hamida Khalil disappeared while that of Huda Shaarawi remained. Class has been a defining key as to who is to be included and who is to be excluded or, rather, forgotten. School books hardly mention any other women who participated in the 1919 Revolution. This can be understood if we recall that these women were defiant of the British and national authorities equally, and the Egyptian Parliament, then, had to be ambivalent about many of their demands.[11] That is to say, recalling the challenging discourse of these women subverts what the state is trying to consolidate. Cultural memory (collective as well but working on the cultural level) took interest recently in these women by republishing their writings and articles and renarrating their stories. It is "an act of transfer,"[12] and it is very close to and sometimes interchangeable with collective memory. It is an act by which groups "constitute their identities by recalling a shared past on the basis of common, and therefore often contested, norms, conventions, and practices."[13] Yet, it is important to say that this is the memory of a certain group; put differently, "every collective memory requires the support of a group delimited in time and space."[14]

In effect, there are several collective memories and one history. In his differentiation of history from memory, Nora reveals the hazards lying behind this process of transformation: "Memory is blind to all but the group it binds." He agrees with Maurice Halbwachs that "there are as many memories as there are groups, that memory is by nature multiple and yet specific; collective, plural, and yet individual." There is one history and multiple memories, and "history is perpetually suspicious of memory and its true mission is to suppress and destroy it."[15]

The multiplicity that characterizes collective memory endorses, then, the concept of diversity. The dominant discourse of power usually propagates one memory, and, in order to enforce this homogeneity, other collective memories must be weakened or be rendered unauthentic. The push and pull between the official memory and the collective memories generates a discursive form of resistance. For instance, when the MB candidate Mohamed Morsi won the presidential elections in 2012, there was an attempt to dismantle the state feminism of Suzanne Mubarak in order to create a new official history. By mere accident, it was discovered that the photo of Doria Shafiq (1908–1975)[16] was deleted from the 2013 to 2014 school-year edition of the national education textbooks for grades eleven and twelve, along with photos of female martyrs from the 25 January Revolution. It turned out that the reason behind this was that "'some religious satellite channels' objected to her not wearing the hijab."[17] The veil triggered another conflict over the photos of female martyrs. Sally Zahran was killed on 28 January 2011, and her photo, where she appears unveiled, was exhibited on posters along with other martyrs. In many locations, Zahran was veiled, either by pen or Photoshopped (as explained in chapter two). The appearance of the martyr became a terrain of conflict over identity and ideology. Precisely, the ensuing conflict centered on how Zahran should be remembered. Walter Armbrust aptly notices that the conflict over Zahran's appearance "functioned as a prism refracting the light of events."[18] The aim was to shift women's agency from autonomous to mediated, and this cannot be done except by a hard intervention in memory so as to redefine women's roles.

This is how memory came to be an arena of political conflict and contesting identity politics. It is this push and pull that has produced what has amounted to a conflict over identity; those in power were seeking a monolithic and fixed identity, while the powerless sought refuge in memory and were seeking a multiple and flexible identity. Perceived as the cultural markers of the nation, women have always been the main factor in this equation and the main tool by which to buttress a certain identity.

Trauma of the 25 January Revolution

Diversity. Freedom. Security. Safety. Decency. Respect. Tolerance. Acceptance. These are the terms that might come close to describing the presence of women in Tahrir Square during the famous eighteen days. Marwa Abdel Samei states that "during the January 25 revolution, Tahrir was represented as the 'virtuous city' where the values of altruism, solidarity, fraternity, dignity, tolerance and coexistence prevailed. It was simply a miniature reflecting the Egypt of which we were all dreaming."[19] To experience such a utopian and euphoric feeling without any prelude is, I believe, highly traumatic. Apparently, this was the case for everybody to the extent that footage and photos of women in Tahrir Square have become fetish locations of memory. The excessive showing of these footage and clips on television has generated a cliché: the role of women in the Revolution. True, but we do not swim in the same river twice.

The Revolution felt like a shock, in other words, the ability to chant out confidently in a high pitch of protest formed what almost resembles a new life, even if it triggered the most aggressive and repressive reactions from the state and its media. Regardless of the consequences, the eighteen days have drawn a demarcating line between a past characterized by repression on the state's part and political inertia on the citizens' part, and a future characterized by the power of the people and a willingness to effect change. Put differently, the 25 January Revolution announced the birth of a new world, politically and discursively. Yet, it was followed immediately by its own crisis. It was a modern moment that generated its own crises (as explained in chapter four), and, in this, it is similar to the trajectory of modernism in the West. While Jurgen Habermas described modernity as "an incomplete project"[20] due to the Surrealists' subversive position toward art and society in the 1920s, likewise, one can safely say that the freedom of expression Egyptians exhibited after the eighteen days formed a shock to Egyptian society. Hence, the rise of a strong conservative discourse—not limited to the MB—that recommends throwing modernity overboard. The inherent repulsive feeling toward any change thrived under the cloak of the call for stability.

The abrupt shift from the highly controlled Mubarak period of thirty years to another that looked completely and loosely liberal was traumatic. And the reaction was highly varied, aggressive, and rapid. Trauma, then, is inherently linked to the shock of modernity, the Revolution in this case. It was experienced as a break in consciousness, which is analogous to the conceptualization of trauma. In his comment on the seminal article of Walter Benjamin "The Work of Art in the Age of Mechanical Reproduction," Kevin Newmark says:

> When the formal patterns of continuity that are presumed to have been grounded in traditional experience by the assimilation of consciousness to memory are disturbed by the truly alien experience of modernity, the coherence of subjective experience is itself displaced in an unexpected way. Consciousness and memory, whatever their relationship in some more or less mythic past, are no longer able to function as associative elements within the same system of individual and collective identity. According to this model, then, modernity would itself be structured like a historical "accident" that has at some prior moment befallen and disrupted the homogenous structure of experience.[21]

Despite the utopian context of the eighteen days, the Revolution threatened to destroy experience in the sense of an integrated or a viable life. The mythic collective identity and the solid imagined community fell apart, allowing several memories to come into play. The historian Dominick LaCapra has distinguished between two kinds of trauma: the first is "historical trauma," which refers to specific, historical occurrences, and the second is "structural trauma," which refers to transhistorical losses, such as entry into language or the inability to partake in a community. For LaCapra, the main difference between these two modes is that historical trauma can be worked through, while structural trauma cannot be healed or changed.[22] One is general and the other is specific to individuals or certain groups. I see the relation between the two modes as somehow blurred, yet both could be discerned in the mapping of the Revolution.

In the context of the Egyptian Revolution, the blurred boundaries between the historical and structural trauma are justified. It is simple: the historical trauma has incurred structural traumas. Without the general, the particular would not have changed; without the radical political change, the personal would have retained the same relation with the world in terms of memory and consciousness. At this juncture of the public and private, or the political and personal, gender is central. In other words, how the eighteen good old days have changed the lives of many women and men personally and epistemologically, forever, is important. But since gender was and still is a contesting, decisive factor in all the trajectories of the Revolution to the extent that it formed essential turning points in the political arena, the link between the political and personal gains priority in women's lives.

Documentations of Memory in Social Media

The awareness of this link between the political and personal was reflected in the rush to document women's experiences. The process of documentation did not spare a single form that could be used. Naturally, alternative and social media turned out to be the most convenient space for embracing all kinds of memories. "Words of Women from the Egyptian Revolution: Herstory to Remind History" was a pioneer project that targeted different ordinary women to document their experiences on YouTube. On its own Facebook page, the project states that it "intends to shed light on and document the participation of women in the Egyptian Revolution and to document their experiences as part of the historical memory."[23] The project has produced ten videos where each video is a profile of a woman filmed with a particular focus on her role in and reaction to the Revolution. Similar short documentaries have been produced by many people who wanted to gauge the meaning and influence of the Revolution on Egyptian women.

However, the most powerful personal and collective locations of memory appeared in the status posted by many on Facebook. The personal status is a space where people can express their views, and it has already become, paradoxically, a contested and contesting space. An example will clarify my point. Ghada Shahbender, a famous activist who cofounded the initiative of Shayfeenkom (We Are Watching You) in 2005 to monitor the elections, uploaded her diaries of January 2011 on her Facebook page. She admits that on 25 January she took to the street as "a compliment to her daughter"; she was afraid of the usual disappointment. In this note, published at the beginning of March 2011, Shahbender elaborates on her feelings in the square, and she is not reticent about her personal fear. In another note, published March 2014, Shahbender tries to explain to a young woman why she cannot go back to what she has described as a "normal life." She declares that since 2005 her life has changed, and she cannot resume the past normality when she enjoyed a sans souci life. The reasons that led to such radical change cover all forms of corruption, political and economic, and clarify how a change in one's view endows one with real agency and determination.[24] In short, 2005 and then 2011 changed Shahbender's life completely. On Facebook, there is a deluge of similar status updates where women's lives have changed due to the 2011 Revolution and where they recall the details as food for thought. In the darkest and most desperate moments, women fall back on memory to derive strength. In the same breath but through a different medium, many women—basically activists, artists, and writers—have published their personal testimonies in journals, magazines, and newspapers to narrate their feelings during the eighteen days (25 January to 11 February). The common feature is that they will never go back to where they were. The memory of January 2011 is not only strongly vivid but also thriving.

Gendered Memory after the Eighteen Days

The cultural memory of the eighteen days was severely shaken. Once the eighteen days were over, this process was extremely problematic. It turned out that the shared past is a myth, and so the act of transfer was governed by "a complex dynamic between past and present, individual and collective, public and private, recall and forgetting, power and powerlessness, history and myth, trauma and nostalgia, conscious and unconscious fears and desires."[25] At some point, this dynamic was transformed into a conflict.

Celebrating International Women's Day (8 March) has always been a shared past. Actually, the whole month of March has been known as the women's month; it comprises International Women's Day, Egyptian Women's Day (16 March), and Mother's Day (21 March). The conspicuous participation of women in the period of the eighteen days, their constant presence that was heavily documented and commented on in the local and international media, the female martyrs, women's testimonies, and their active role that was not mediated through men meant that there was going to be a new Egypt for the new woman. Naturally, everybody expected that celebrating International Women's Day on 8 March 2011 was bound to take a different form and significance. That is to say, the concerned women—now political players—were the ones who were going to celebrate in their own words, not in the words of the NCW as usual. Therefore, the women who faced the tear gas along with men during the eighteen days and who were stalwart participants in toppling Mubarak planned for a million-women march on that day. Shamefully, the march was intimidated, and the gathering was met with heckling and abuse. Ahmad Awadalla, an eyewitness, tried to defend the women, and the countermob said to him, "Why are you defending women? Are you queer?"[26] The mob kept attacking the women's gathering until the military dispersed the whole crowd.

This incident brings into focus the role of cultural memory. The time span between 11 February and 8 March is very short, and this is where the danger lies. The bad memories of the Algerian Revolution come to one's mind immediately. Algerian women participated with men in combating the French occupation, and the moment of gaining independence meant sending the women back to their homes. Yet, women's participation in that Algerian Revolution was mediated through male designation,[27] which was not the case with Egyptian women. What happened on that day was the initiation of a cracked and disrupted cultural memory that worked against women. The situation on that day was highly dialectical in relation to cultural memory, since promoting women's rights has always been linked to the ex-regime or, rather, to what Hoda Elsadda calls "the first lady syndrome."[28] Therefore, those who attacked the women's march were not willing to recall the memory of those past days. On the other side, the women's memory of the eighteen days was still alive and fresh, and so it was taken for granted that lobbying for their rights was part and parcel of those days. Sadly enough, all aspirations of gender equality were severely crushed and most of the ensuing headlines screamed this. Celebrating International Women's Day became a signifier of the old regime, and the crowd decided to challenge it. From the perspective of the women, celebrating it was a signifier of restoring their voice, and the hostile reaction they were met with signified a return to dystopia. This was the first gendered conflict between memory and countermemory—revolution and counterrevolution could be equivalent terms.

Less than twenty-four hours later, another catastrophe took place, only to escalate the conflict. A sit-in in Tahrir Square was dispersed forcefully by the military; young women and men were detained and tortured in the Egyptian Museum, and eighteen women were taken into military detention for four days. Some of them told Amnesty International that during that time male soldiers beat them, gave them electric shocks, and subjected them to strip searches.[29] They were then forced to undergo a series of virginity tests in full view of the soldiers and threatened with prostitution charges. Before they were released, the women were brought before a military court and received one-year suspended sentences for a variety of concocted charges. This incident has been widely and internationally condemned and taken as a material proof that the Revolution has generated a gender paradox.[30] One is tempted to analyze the complicated implications of this shameful, abusive act; however, it has already been read and reread to reveal how society was not willing to accommodate women's rights, especially in relation to the female body (detailed in chapter four). What concerns me here is how this incident has played an important role, not only in the formation and disruption of cultural memory but also in the trajectory of political memory, which makes gender a subtext[31] in the Revolution.

While most of the detained women chose to resort to silence, only one, Samira Ibrahim, chose to file a lawsuit against SCAF. Her courage was shockingly subversive in a society that has learnt not to break silence over the question of the female body. Moreover, she was highly slandered and vilified, even accused of lying. Throughout a long tedious process, Ibrahim came out both victorious and defeated. On 11 March 2012, a not guilty verdict was delivered against the doctor who conducted this shameful act. It is important that the timing of the verdict coincided with the celebrations of International Women's Day and Egyptian Women's Day. Yet, her decision to break the silence surely changed the old paternal logic. On the occasion of the second anniversary of the Revolution, *Jadaliyya* launched a series of articles, among which Sherine Seikaly wrote an article titled "The Meaning of Revolution: On Samira Ibrahim," where she concluded that Ibrahim "did not claim the category of the Virgin as a sacred space of refuge. She did not fight her brutalization in the tired terms of honor and righteousness. She fought it on political grounds."[32] Ibrahim became, indeed, an iconic woman, recalled in different times and forms to protest against the military.

The initial traumatic effect of this horrendous abuse was mitigated by a revolutionary sociopolitical discourse that holds any power complicit with the military accountable. The incident has been (and still is) employed as a hard reminder of the violations committed by the SCAF, of the high price women have paid, of the perverted measures taken against protesters, and of the responsibility of many political actors. The virginity tests, along with the incident of the girl who was stripped to her blue bra[33] by the military in November 2011, are recalled again and again as acts of memory that could take the form of "performance, representation, and interpretation," as Hirsch and Smith have termed them. They have also confirmed that these acts of memory—what this book refers to as 'reminders'—require "agents and specific contexts. They can be conscious and deliberate; at the same time, and this is certainly true in the case of trauma, they can be involuntary, repetitious, obsessive."[34] Protesters, both men and women, managed to turn these two atrocious incidents into tools of resistance, and, thus, they merged the female body into the body politic to engrave a new revolutionary memory that does not lock violence against women into the private, personal, and the unsaid.

Street art has proven itself to be the best medium of challenge and resistance to any hegemonic discourse. In addition to declaring positions, articulating demands, and protesting violations, street art revives memory, even if intermittently. Interestingly enough, the street art related to Samira Ibrahim developed in a similar way to the development of the case, discursively and legally. At the very beginning and when Ibrahim filed a lawsuit against the officers, she was glorified as a courageous person; that was reflected in her stenciled portrait on walls, without any captions. Then, her stencil appeared above the military as a reminder of the protesters' defiance of the military, to which later was added some hieroglyphic letters, which brought in the question of identity. This evolution of the new text proves that there was a discourse in the making; it was a discourse that was rereading its own givens and weaving its fabric out of direct reality. Moreover, it was a discourse that had its underpinning in identity, and gender identity was essential at that moment. Identity, whether individual or cultural, becomes "a story that stretches from the past to the present and the future, that connects the individual to the group, and that is structured by gender and related identity markers."[35] With the legal close of the case, Ibrahim's graffiti appeared with the caption "you cannot break me," in imitation of the banner she was carrying in front of the court on the day of the trial.

The drawings moved gradually from the individual to the collective, from the particular to the general, from the temporal to the political, and from the abrupt and traumatic to the deliberate and conscious. Samira Ibrahim's portraits on the walls took another turn when they were merged with two figures: the first was that of Khaled Said, the photos of whose tortured corpse helped spark the Revolution with the Facebook page titled "We Are All Khaled Said"; and the second was that of Alia Mahdi who published her nude photos on her blog and caused widespread uproar. In their attempts to engrave a countermemory, the protesters decided to confront previous charges of immorality that were hurled at them when Mahdi uploaded her photos. This interpretation and representation of memory is extremely problematic. To lavish virtue on Samira Ibrahim, Mahdi had to be vilified on the walls. This compare-and-contrast method cannot be even taken as a dialectic; it is a form of ambivalence toward gender. While Ibrahim was turned by collective memory into a political protester, Mahdi was turned into a frivolous woman. To juxtapose the political and the personal through the female body meant a return to square one. It is also an example of how memory can work against itself in specific contexts. These drawings play on the dynamics of memory, and they all facilitate reading the development and problematics of a newly born gender discourse.

The development of these drawings proves that Samira Ibrahim's case was not perceived as an aberration; on the contrary, it was contextualized in the fabric of a long memory of atrocities so as to render the virginity tests part and parcel of a long series of repressive measures. The fact that Ibrahim's images on the walls of the city engaged with a network of meanings culturally and politically shows how a certain traumatic defining experience of gender has been circulated widely and transformed radically. The associations of such a shameful violation have extended far beyond the personal, down to the memory of Khaled Said, and, thus, they were located in a political continuum. Discursively, the drawings functioned as a reminder of the brutality of the authoritarian military and, therefore, protesting against this power was (and still is) justified.

The woman who was stripped to her blue bra in November 2011 sparked the same memory, only to show that the memory of protesters was accumulative. Despite her complete silence (her identity was never revealed) that stands in stark opposition to Ibrahim's defiance, this woman was again turned into an icon of gender that empowered the memory of protest. The million-women march that was planned in solidarity with the woman who is commonly known as 'the blue bra girl' was nothing less than a grand performance. It is important to remember that acts of memory are "acts of performance, representation, and interpretation."[36] The thousands of women, surrounded by a quasi-human shield of men who provided a symbolic act of solidarity and protection, chanting to the rhythm of drums were a perfect reenactment and commemoration of another atrocity. The chants were important: the first was "women of Egypt are a red line," later co-opted by the Muslim Sisters, and the second was in itself a revival of memory: "*Irfa'i rasek, enti ashraf men eli dasek*" (Hold your head up, you are more honorable than he who trampled you). While the former was a variation on the concept of 'red lines' (taboos), the latter was chanted for Ibrahim when she came out of court, itself a variation on the chant that was resonating in Tahrir Square after the departure of Mubarak: "*Irfaʻ rasak foʼ, enta masri*" (Hold your head up, you are Egyptian).

The incident of the blue bra girl introduced into the poignant political scene a new factor: that of the dialectic between absence and presence. In spite of the girl's silence, she gained a remarkable presence through the acts of memory. And, while several photos became symbolic, the girl's photo that was held in Tahrir Square the next day became "a flesh-and-blood human being who becomes virtual and goes viral, returning within a few days to haunt the real space of Tahrir Square as the banner of the Egyptian women's movement," as W.J.T. Mitchell has noticed.[37] Actually, it returned to occupy several places in different forms, and graffiti was one of them. The drawing reenacts the incident literally, with all its brutality. It is a form of solidarity, reflected highly in chants, that is bent on smashing the paradigm of shame and guilt. With this incident, it became apparent that the conflict was over the categorization of the assaults; the regressive traditional camp wanted to lock and locate these abuses in the personal and private, while the revolutionary camp pushed it forward, through acts of memory, to the political and public, insisting that the personal is political and cultural (and it has always been so). Yet, we should take into consideration that reviving the memory of this brutality contributed to undermining and contesting the structure of the authoritarian rule of SCAF. Similar to colonialism, SCAF created subjects "who are almost the same but not quite,"[38] and it is in this difference that subversion and resistance are located. The constant remembering of these violations that are related to women's bodies was a tool of resistance and defiance. Despite the apology of SCAF, the dynamics of forgetting were much weaker than those of remembering.

During December 2012, when Morsi was in power, a sit-in in front of the Presidential Palace was stormed by pro-MB Islamists, where several activists were literally kidnapped, tortured for hours, and, then, handed in to the police. Among those kidnapped was Ola Shahba, a leftist female activist. She was severely beaten at the outset when she was mistaken for a man (because of the helmet on her head); she was then sexually harassed and incarcerated in a kiosk for twelve hours. In her testimony, Shahba narrated all the physical and verbal violations committed against her. It should be noted that gender was one of the determining factors in Shahba's experience. To clarify, the moment her kidnappers realized that she was a woman, they shifted from hitting her on the head to slapping and verbally harassing her. When they started touching her body she screamed, "Do not touch me," upon which the leader slapped her again for such "an accusation."[39] However, although Shahba's testimony is forcefully transmitted through her own voice and body, it does not mean that she speaks of her own memory. Halbwachs has pointed out that "it is in society that people normally acquire their memories. It is also in society that they recall, recognize, and localize their memories."[40] Therefore, Shahba's shock, as shown in her testimony, was triggered by another memory. The Islamists who were slapping and torturing her were her comrades in the square during the eighteen days. Politics, then, was another key factor in Shahba's trauma. When she testified to the fact that her kidnappers dealt with her as a left-wing enemy, the dominant story of the Tahrir utopia fell apart. The importance of the testimony stems from the fact that it is a reminder that power insulates itself from all previous alliances. Yet, interestingly enough, Shahba's testimony angered the kidnappers only because she mentioned sexual harassment. In other words, the testimony of the individual and its reception exhibit different epistemological standpoints and positions.

Shattering the Silence of the Body

The horrific rise of sexual harassment incidents that targeted female protesters brought the realization that women's bodies have become the place of gender victimization. The harassed body is turned into the means by which gender becomes "performative," or as Judith Butler explains: "Such acts, gestures, enactments, generally construed, are *performative* in the sense that the essence or identity that they otherwise purport to express are *fabrications* manufactured and sustained through corporeal signs and other discursive means."[41] The act of harassment, then, is one of the most traumatic forms of 'gender trouble' where the female body is enforced into a certain category of gender that emanates from inequalities of sex.

Extremely challenging culturally and psychologically, the crisis represented a crossroads for the new discourse that was busy repositioning gender into the political scene. The position taken toward such sustained acts of harassment could have either pushed the new discourse beyond gender, or it could have dragged it backward to relocate gender in the old logic of binaries where sex and gender are indistinct.

Several campaigns were launched to help women deal with (and to protect them where possible from) these horrific mob assaults.[42] Since resorting to silence was the expected reaction, breaking it was quite a challenge. That is to say, a huge corpus of testimonial literature turned such a traumatic experience into a psychological and discursive tool of resistance. More importantly, documenting the experience of harassment became part of documenting the Revolution. Paul Ricoeur has stated that "we must not forget that everything starts, not from the archives, but from testimony, and that . . . we have nothing better than testimony, in the final analysis, to assure ourselves that something did happen in the past."[43] These testimonies integrated the politics of the body into the body politic. Narrative, as an act of memory, becomes an act of interpretation and a means of working through something. LaCapra explains that this act helps the harassed to

> work through posttraumatic symptoms in the present in a manner that opens possible futures. It also enables one to recount events and perhaps evoke experience, typically through nonlinear movements that allow trauma to register in language and its hesitations, indirections, pauses, and silences. And particularly, by bearing witness and giving testimony, narrative may help performatively to create openings in existence that did not exist before.[44]

The testimonies, then, as acts of memory, are performative and interpretive. These testimonies, some of which were really frightening, were circulated widely on various social media platforms, gained wide readership, and snowballed anger. At the same time, they provided a way to cure the victim by rendering the inaudible into the audible. At this juncture of the personal, individual, female body, silence and public, social, body politic, and memory, the harassed women could start the way toward the healing process through integrating their traumatic experience into collective memory.

True, silence on questions of gendered violence was shattered by narrating the act of harassment. Yet, we should remember some of the drawbacks that underlie the narration of experience, even if it is a testimony. Joan W. Scott warns that "the project of making experience visible precludes analysis of the workings of this system and of its historicity; instead it reproduces its terms." Scott has every right to warn, so the testimonies "expose the existence of repressive mechanisms, but not their inner workings or logic." What is needed is "to attend to the historical processes that, through discourse, position subjects and produce their experiences."[45] The discursive framework from within which the campaigns worked depended on several factors. First, they historicized the use of sexual harassment as a weapon against women in all political protests, thus reviving the memory of the past. The historical contextualization of these incidents was another act of memory that revealed the mechanics of the regime in turning the female body into a tool of discipline and punishment. Second, the details of the testimonies focused on the discourse of the harasser where he (or they) used sexist terms, which revealed how gender was a determining factor in the conflict. Third, the testimonies of the harassed revealed awareness that the female body was used as a weapon to incur shame and incite fear; this awareness made the women realize that a specific gender identity was 'fabricated,' to use Butler's term,[46] and enforced on them.

One cannot read the testimonies of harassed women in isolation from the context and location. To explain, sexual harassment is not a new phenomenon, yet its systematic rise in locations of protest endows it with a completely different meaning. There is no doubt that sexual harassment, physically and verbally, has become a weapon of terrorization, carried out and organized by certain powers that believe gender is the most fragile factor by which women could be deterred from the public sphere. That the testimonies were far from being self-indicting and that the testifiers were not deterred from going back to the struggle (solidarity and campaigning cannot be overlooked) are huge achievements, especially when

compared to the consequences of the similar events in 2005.[47] The hor-
rifying testimonies published on the websites of several initiatives and
organizations helped to convince many that sexual harassment is not the
fault of the woman; on the contrary, it is viewed as a criminal act that
aims at humiliating and reifying the female body so as to abort women's
agency. This is exactly where the women managed to turn the personal
into the political. Put differently, at the juncture of the private and public,
women's testimonies stand distinguished from all other testimonies. This
is because they engaged with what has always been perceived as a taboo.
The testimonies proved that "there is a direct relation . . . between soci-
ality and subjectivity, between language and consciousness, or between
institutions and individuals."[48]

Another drawback of narrating trauma is what Cathy Caruth describes
as a "loss." The transformation of the trauma into a narrative memory, in
other words, a testimony that allows the story to be communicated and
integrated into the individual and collective knowledge of the past might
lead to losing

> both the precision and the force that characterizes traumatic
> recall. . . . Yet, beyond the loss of precision, there is another, more
> profound, disappearance: the loss, precisely, of the event's essen-
> tial incomprehensibility, the force of its *affront to understanding*.[49]

LaCapra has taken issue with this statement and argued that
"working-through need not be understood to imply the integration or
transformation of past trauma into a seamless narrative memory and total
meaning or knowledge."[50] For him, testifying to the present opens up
possible futures. And this is exactly what happened as a result of the testimonial literature narrated by harassed women. The politics of forgetting
and silencing the harassed female body were completely subverted.
Through memory, women's bodies gained the status of a main political
actor, and there was no return to silence. The fact that many institutions and activists are engaged in combating sexual harassment proves
LaCapra's belief that testimonies open up new future horizons. Without
these testimonies, silence would have remained as the norm.

Historical Memory

This section looks at the way certain ideas—turned into images, whether physical or mental—serve the memory of and about gender. Roland Barthes's notion of "punctum" is useful in this context and can render a feminist reading of the appearance of the past in the present.[51] Following Barthes, we can say that some remnants give information about the past, while others prick and puncture memory to expose the unexpected, in other words, what lies out of the frame of the image. The punctum is a point of memory that is strictly personal, and, yet, it intersects with the cultural and historical only to render the elusive question of gender visible. While the punctum, for Barthes, is a detail that he alone notices because of some personal connection, we have to remember that this detail is also always derived from a cultural and historical repertoire. Otherwise, he would not have noticed it. At this juncture of the personal and cultural, memory transmission takes place. In both of these ways, personal and cultural, objects and images inherited from the past can keep the gender issue alive in cultural memory. Yet, Barthes does not stop at that. He elaborates his discussion of the punctum and gives it another meaning. He says: "I now know that there exists another punctum (another 'stigmatum') than the 'detail.' This new punctum, which is no longer of form but of intensity, is Time, the lacerating emphasis of *noeme* ('that-has-been'), its pure representation."[52] The punctum of time refers to the wide gap between the meaning of an object or image, then, and the meaning it holds now when it comes back to life through the transmission of memory. Most importantly, this gap points at the inevitability of loss, death, and change.[53] The two examples I am going to read as acts of transmission highlight how an image is turned into a cultural and historical punctum and a punctum of time as well.

"I have opened the floodgates": this is the slogan of the Fuada Watch initiative that appears alongside a photo of the famous Egyptian actress Shadia. Fuada is a character engraved in popular memory; she is the heroine of the Egyptian classic film *Shay min al-khouf* (Something to fear), released in 1969 and inspired by Tharwat Abaza's short story with the same title. In the story, Atris, a despot, punished the inhabitants of a village by closing off access to a river, leaving them and their plants to die. Fuada, a simple girl, was meant to be married, against her will, to Atris. Yet she was the only one brave enough in the village to break the blockade, allowing water to flow and drench the dry land. We should remember that toward the end of the film, all the villagers stage a march to Atris's house, chanting, "The marriage of Atris and Fuada is annulled." This chant has gone through critical phases in the cultural memory of Egypt: a breakthrough, something kitsch, a joke, and a remote past. The resurrection of Fuada's image and words, modified significantly into "I have opened the floodgates of freedom," in post-revolutionary Egypt, precisely in 2012, has crucial implications in the devastating disjunctions between past and present. The words—along with the chant of the villagers resonating in the reader's mind—glorify the protagonist as a heroic figure who liberated the village through the metaphorical act of opening the floodgates. Put differently, she initiated an act of regeneration and fertility. Therefore, the protagonist, Fuada, carries multiple cultural and historical layers; consequently, her image, coming back in 2012, functions as a punctum of time. With the rise of the violations of women's rights, the chant and the words alternatively have become a sign of protest. Resurrecting a remote memory is in itself, in this particular context, a countermemory. In addition to being a punctum, the image of Fuada with the famous slogan turns protest into a performance replete with hope. Fuada Watch is an initiative that was founded to call for boycotting the vote on the 2012 constitution due to the articles that violate women's rights. The message is clear: Fuada brings back and revives the act of resistance and defiance.

A second example is that of the crescent and the cross. During the 1919 Egyptian Revolution, when a flag was used as a symbol of the Egyptian nation, it was often the flag of the crescent and the cross where the crescent, the symbol of Islam, and the cross, the symbol of Christianity, were drawn side by side, with the former embracing the latter. (The cross was not clearly represented, in other words, it was closer to the shape of a star.) The flag, thus, was a vivid visualization of transsectarian solidarity in defiance of British control of Egypt. Later, it became the badge of the nationalist Wafd Party, which dominated Egyptian politics until the early 1950s. It is worth noting that, in many of the existing photographs of the demonstrations of 1919, it is often women who carry these flags of the crescent and the cross.[54]

The same visual symbol was strongly recalled during the 2011 Revolution to symbolize that the whole country had joined forces against the government and, also, to eliminate the official discourse that was inciting fear in Copts. The adoption of slogans and symbols of Muslim–Christian unity is particularly important in a context where the Coptic community had been the target of a long series of deadly attacks. The unity, shown in banners, flags, and graffiti, was meant to subvert the state's manipulation of the feelings of minorities. These symbols were all accompanied by the slogans *kollena eid wahda* (we are all one hand) or *kollena did al-nizam* (we are all against the regime). The significance of this form of memory revival was apparent in the people's and the regime's mind equally. Cultural memory has always retained that symbol as a sign of resistance, and, thus, its revival as a signifier in a specific context implies that the signified is defiance. The memory of 1919 was valorized in 2011, in a context where "identity is problematized."[55]

However, when it turned out that the political atmosphere was not in favor of Copts' rights, the slogan of the crescent and cross came back again in the most personal and unexpected form: a silver necklace that comprises the crescent intertwining the cross. This was in reaction to the discrimination against Copts. As part of their will to fight for their rights and to claim individuality, Egyptian women decided to turn the most political into the most personal. Therefore, wearing this necklace was not only a sign of defying the fundamentalist discourse and of expressing transsectarian solidarity but also a sign of asserting "the power of presence," as Asef Bayat terms it.[56] The necklace, then, has become a punctum of memory; it revives a point in time that was stuffed with layers of political and cultural significations. To turn this punctum into a personal sign is a form of articulating the past when identity was the main problematic player. Simultaneously, wearing the necklace exemplifies "collective action by non-collective actors."[57] Women made their presence highly visible through resorting to ordinary activities and the practices of everyday life. It is in the daily micropolitics and extreme ordinariness that women were capable of asserting their vision by bringing the personal into the political. In other words, women managed to manipulate memory for their own benefit.

Things are not as easy and smooth as they seem. Wulf Kansteiner's critique of collective memory is useful here. According to Kansteiner, collective memory represents a complex process of cultural interaction and negotiation between three historical tropes: the visual and discursive objects of memory, memory makers, and memory consumers.[58] It is that last factor that is not studied enough, although it is the problematic one. It is precisely memory consumers "who often read memorial artifacts against the grain of their intended meaning."[59] This brings to the fore another dialectic. Memory transmitters assume the existence of a stable interpretive community, which is far from the truth. A personal anecdote might explain what I mean. I have been wearing the crescent and cross necklace for a long time. My intention was to express solidarity with the Copts and to declare my position. Many assume that I am a Copt, and, thus, they treat me accordingly: either positively or negatively. The intended meaning never comes through. Over and above, it turned out that not all of us share the same memory, and, hence, there is the question: Why are you wearing a cross? There are many other examples where the artistic or historical punctum has turned into a marker of political memory; they all depend on a shared past that takes a new meaning in the present. In a nutshell, women activists managed to capitalize on the historical memory that is shared by society members and turned it into a medium through which lobbying and protesting were facilitated.

Then What?

While memory has clearly become a central concept in the revolutionary act, it is equally threatened with erasure by the discourse of any authoritarian regime under the cover of forgiving and starting afresh. That usually takes the form of emotional and rational blackmail exercised by power to find a safe exit. Yet, the politics of forgiving are always conflated with the politics of forgetting. This is where the real challenge lies, and, apparently, the only way out is to work on the archives, in their multifarious forms, to prevent the powerful from selecting and deleting. Archiving and documenting are the two safeguards of collective memory. On the other side, memory consumers should be taken into consideration, since they are the party who can protect memory from being deformed by the historical record. Documenting atrocities committed against women should be part and parcel of documenting the Revolution. Merging the two together is bound to yield a process of memory construction.

NOTES

Introduction

1   Kumari Jayawardena, *Feminism and Nationalism in the Third World* (London: Zed Books, 1986). This book is widely used in women and gender studies around the world. As an oft-cited work that has gained international recognition, the book was chosen for the Feminist Fortnight Award in Britain in 1986.

2   Hannah Arendt, *The Human Condition* (Chicago: Chicago University Press, 1958), 199.

3   Asef Bayat, *Life as Politics: How Ordinary People Change the Middle East*, ISIM Series on Contemporary Muslim Societies (Amsterdam: Amsterdam University Press, 2010), 97.

4   Nicola Pratt, "Egyptian Women: Between Revolution, Counter-Revolution, Orientalism, and 'Authenticity,'" *Jadaliyya*, 6 May 2013, http://www.jadaliyya.com/pages/index/11559/egyptian-women_between-revolution-counter

5   Deniz Kandiyoti, "Disquiet and despair: The gender sub-texts of the 'Arab Spring,'" *Open Democracy*, 26 June 2012, http://www.opendemocracy.net/print/66458

6   Sharon Marcus, "Fighting Bodies, Fighting Words: A Theory and Politics of Rape Prevention," *Feminists Theorize the Political*, edited by Judith Butler and Joan W. Scott (London: Routledge, 1992), 394.

7   Audre Lorde, "The Master's Tools Will Never Dismantle the Master's House," *Feminist Postcolonial Theory: A Reader*, edited by Reina Lewis and Sara Mills (Edinburgh: Edinburgh University Press, 2003), 379.

8   Susan Stanford Friedman, *Mappings: Feminism and the Cultural Geographies of Encounter* (Princeton: Princeton University Press, 1998), 17–35.

9   Bayat, *Life as Politics*, 97.

10 Michel Foucault, *Discipline and Punishment: The Birth of the Prison* (New York: Random House, 1975), 138.

11 Judith Butler, *Gender Trouble: Feminism and the Subversion of Identity* (London: Routledge, 1999), 173.

12 Marianne Hirsch and Valerie Smith, "'Feminism and Cultural Memory': An Introduction," *Signs: Journal of Women in Culture and Society* 28, no. 1 (Fall 2002): 5.

Notes to Chapter 1

1   Hossam el-Hamalawy, "Revolt in Mahalla," *International Socialist Review* 59, (May–June 2008).

2   Asmaa Mahfouz (b. 1985) is an Egyptian activist and one of the founders of the 6 April Youth Movement. She helped spark the mass protests with the video she uploaded on her blog one week before 25 January 2011.

3   Lila Abu-Lughod and Rabab El-Mahdi, "Beyond the 'Woman Question' in the Egyptian Revolution." *Feminist Studies* 37, no. 3 (Fall 2011): 684.

4   The elites of the regime were those who supported the discourse of Mubarak and defended the extreme measures taken by the security forces. They worked hard to endow the regime with legitimacy. Starting from 2011, they have been referred to as *folool* ('remnants' of the former regime).

5   Anne McClintock, "'No Longer in a Future Heaven': Gender, Race, and Nationalism," in *Dangerous Liaisons: Gender, Nation, and Postcolonial Perspectives*, edited by Anne McClintock, Aamir Mufti, and Ella Shohat (Minneapolis: University of Minnesota Press, 1997), 89.

6   Hoda Elsadda, "Egypt: The Battle over Hope and Morale," *Open Democracy*, 2 November 2011.

7   Abu-Lughod and El-Mahdi, "Beyond the 'Woman Question,'" 685.

8   Deniz Kandiyoti, ed, *Women, Islam and the State* (London: Macmillan, 1991), 8. Sherine Hafez has employed the same concept aptly in her research to understand the politics of feminism in post-Revolution Egypt, see "Gender and Citizenship Center Egypt: Sondra Hale's Legacy and Egypt's Ongoing Revolution," *Journal of Middle East Women's Studies* 10, no. 1 (Winter 2010): 82–100.

9   Benedict Anderson, *Imagined Communities: Reflections on the Origin and Spread of Nationalism* (London: Verso, 1983).

10 Nadje Al-Ali, *Secularism, Gender, and the State in the Middle East* (Cambridge: Cambridge University Press, 2000), 46.

11 Leila Abouzeid, *Year of the Elephant: A Moroccan Woman's Journey Toward Independence and Other Stories*, translated by Barbara Parmenter (Cairo: American University of Cairo Press, 1989), 1.

12 Kumari Jayawardena, *Feminism and Nationalism in the Third World* (London: Zed Press, 1986).

13   Kandiyoti, ed, *Women, Islam, and the State*; Beth Baron, *The Women's Awakening in Egypt: Culture, Society, and the Press* (New Haven, CT: Yale University Press, 1984); Mervat Hatem, "The Pitfalls of the Nationalist Discourses on Citizenship," *Gender and Citizenship in the Middle East*, edited by S. Joseph, (Syracuse, NY: Syracuse University Press, 2000), 33–57; Al-Ali, *Secularism, Gender, and the State*; Leila Ahmed, *Women and Gender and Islam: Historical Roots of a Modern Debate* (New Haven: Yale University Press, 1992).

14   Hala Kamal, "Inserting Women's Rights in the Egyptian Constitution," *Journal for Cultural Research* (2015): doi: 10.1080/14797585.2014.982919

15   A few MPs refused to stand during the national anthem, and others supported the idea of calling for prayers during the sessions.

16   Translation by the author.

17   Anne McClintock, "'No Longer in a Future Heaven,'" 90.

18   With the arrival of General Abd al-Fattah al-Sisi, women were a main component of his discourse. He, repeatedly, thanked them in his speeches and, later, implied that they were the guardians of the nation.

19   Rajia Omran is a lawyer and activist. She is also one of the founders of No to Military Trials.

20   Susan Stanford Friedman, *Mappings: Feminism and the Cultural Geographies of Encounter* (Princeton, NJ: Princeton University Press, 1998), 90.

21   Julian Henriques et al, *Changing the Subject: Psychology, Social Regulation and Subjectivity* (London: Methuen, 1984), 117.

22   Bronwyn Davies, "The Concept of Agency: A Feminist Poststructuralist Analysis," *The International Journal of Social and Cultural Practices*, no. 30 (December 1991): 43.

23   Michel Foucault, *Discipline and Punishment: The Birth of the Prison* (New York: Random House, 1975).

24   Friedman, *Mappings*, 19.

25   Friedman, *Mappings*, 19.

26   Friedman provides a long endnote where she explains that gynocriticism is a neologism that was advanced by Elaine Showalter in 1979, whereas 'gynesis' is another term that was advanced by Alice Jardine in 1982, and Showalter used it to describe the poststructuralist readings of the feminine (244). I am adapting both terms, however, to refer to certain methodologies used widely in analyzing women's position. Analysts used to look for women's participation and presence and women's discourse as signs of women's empowerment regardless of the problematic identity politics.

27   Friedman, *Mappings*, 20–25.

28   Friedman, *Mappings*, 20.

29   Friedman, *Mappings*, 19.

30   I was among those left angry, and this position, along with my leftist leanings, branded me 'indifferent' toward terrorism.

31   Friedman, *Mappings*, 24.
32   Nadje Al-Ali, "Feminist Dilemmas in (Counter-) Revolutionary Egypt,"
     NORA—Nordic Journal of Feminist and Gender Research 21, no. 4 (2013):
     312–316, doi: 10.1080/08038740.2013.854274
33   Friedman, *Mappings*, 89.
34   Davies, "The Concept of Agency," 51.
35   Friedman, *Mappings*, 31.
36   Friedman, *Mappings*, 5.
37   Friedman, *Mappings*, 7.
38   Mervat Hatem, "Gender and Revolution in Egypt," *Middle East Report* 261
     (Winter 2011): 36–41.
39   Friedman, *Mappings*, 35.

Notes to Chapter 2

1   Bill Ashcroft, "Conflict and Transformation," *The IAFOR Journal of Litera-
    ture and Librarianship* 3, no. 1(Winter 2014): 1.
2   Edward Said, *The World, the Text, and the Critic* (Cambridge, MA: Harvard
    UP, 1983). Said insists that writing is an event that takes place in the world,
    and it acts as a material force that effects and affects.
3   In a discussion with Professor Handel Wright that took place at the con-
    ference of "Multiculturalism: Theories and Practices" held by Cardiff
    University in May 2012, he suggested that the terms "diversity" and "differ-
    ences" are more applicable to the Egyptian case than "multicultural."
4   Jurgen Habermas, "Modernity – An Incomplete Project," *The Anti-Aes-
    thetic: Essays on Postmodern Culture*, edited by Hal Foster (New York: The
    New Press, 1998), 3.
5   It should be noted here that the term 'generation' does not indicate any age
    markers; it signifies a new mindset that was fueled and motivated by the
    revolutionary act.
6   The avant-garde is used in this context to refer to a militant rising generation,
    similar in its discursive practice to the 1920s avant-garde, yet it does not adopt
    a Leninist orientation or a Surrealist dimension. It is avant-garde coming of
    age in a new place and time. At the same time, it fiercely opposes a strong
    arrière-garde, in other words, all the Old Guards who support the counter-
    revolution, whether the military, Islamists, or those who were part and parcel
    of the ex-regime. Therefore, this new avant-garde is always belligerent.
7   Habermas, "Modernity," 4.
8   This chant rhymes in Arabic, and, apparently, nothing of it has been
    achieved until now.
9   Anne McClintock, "'No Longer in a Future Heaven': Gender, Race,
    and Nationalism," in *Dangerous Liaisons: Gender, Nation, and Postcolonial
    Perspectives*, edited by Anne McClintock, Aamir Mufti, and Ella Shohat
    (Minneapolis: University of Minnesota Press, 1997).

10   Deniz Kandiyoti, Guest Editor's Introduction to "The Awkward Relationship: Gender and Nationalism," *Nations and Nationalism* 6 (2000): 491.

11   Cornel West, "The New Cultural Politics of Difference," *The Cultural Studies Reader*, edited by Simon During (London: Routledge, 1993), 213.

12   Walter Benjamin, *Illuminations: Essays and Reflections*, edited by Hannah Arendt, translated by Harry Zohn (New York: Schocken Books, 1968).

13   Gerald Raunig, *Art and Revolution, Transversal Activism in the Long Twentieth Century* (New York: Semiotext(e), 2007), 18.

14   Yet, the term 'transversality' was first developed by Félix Guattari in 1964 as a result of his experience at La Borde clinic in France. His theory takes as its point of departure the forced relationship "between the world of the insane and the rest of society" and the need to avoid at any cost taking the object of institutional therapy "out of the real context of society." Guattari sought to introduce open collective practices that worked across the confines of the institution itself. He explains that "transversality contrasts with—verticality, such as one finds in the representative structure of a pyramid (president, vice-president, etc.); and—horizontality, which can prevail in a hospital courtyard, in the department of the restless or the bedwetters, in other words in a condition where people make do as best as they can with the situation in which they find themselves," *The Guattari Reader*, edited by Gary Genosko (Oxford: Blackwell, 1996), 14–16.

15   Raunig, *Art and Revolution*, 18.

16   Susan Kelly, "The Transversal and the Invisible: How Do You Really Make a Work of Art That Is Not a Work of Art?" *Republic Art*, January 2005, http://www.republicart.net/disc/mundial/kelly01_en.htm_

17   Michel Foucault, "The Subject and Power," *Critical Inquiry* 8, no. 4 (Summer 1982): 777–95.

18   Stuart Hall, "The Local and the Global: Globalization and Ethnicity," *Dangerous Liaisons: Gender, Nation, and Postcolonial Perspectives*, edited by Anne McClintock, Aamir Mufti, and Ella Shohat (Minneapolis: University of Minnesota Press, 1997), 183.

19   Hall, "The Local and the Global," 183.

20   Raunig, *Art and Revolution*, 49.

21   Foucault, "The Subject and Power," 780.

22   Asef Bayat, *Life as Politics: How Ordinary People Change the Middle East*, ISIM Series on Contemporary Muslim Societies (Amsterdam: Amsterdam University Press, 2010), 98.

23   Mona Abaza, "Intimidation and Resistance: Imagining Gender in Cairene Graffiti," *Al Ahram Weekly*, 2 July 2013.

24   "Revolution, Turmoil Impact on Egypt's Pop Culture," *Ahram Online*, 3 January 2014.

25   On TED website: Bahia Shehab, "The new revolution in Egypt and why I wanted to feminize it: An essay," 5 July 2013, http://blog.ted.com/the-new-revolution-in-egypt-and-why-i-wanted-to-feminize-it-an-essay/

http://fellowsblog.ted.com/2013/07/05/ the-new-revolution-in-egypt-and-why-i-wanted-to-feminize-it-an-essay

26   Friedman, *Mappings*, 19.

27   Hannah Elansary, "Revolutionary Street Art: Complicating the Discourse," *Ahram Online*, 3 September 2014, http://english.ahram.org.eg/NewsContent/5/35/109860/Arts--Culture/Stage--Street/Revolutionary-Street-Art-Complicating-the-Discours.aspx

28   Michel de Certeau, *The Practice of Everyday Life* (Berkeley: University of California Press, 1984), xiii.

29   Quoted by Rowan El Shimi in "Segn Al-Nesa: Ramadan TV Hit Offers Glimpse of Life in Women's Prison," *Ahram Online*, 21 July 2014.

30   *Al Hayat*, 19 August 2014.

31   In October 2015, a Google search of "Sally Zahran" yielded 9,010 images.

32   Walter Armbrust, "The Ambivalence of Martyrs and the Counter-revolution," Fieldsights —Hot Spots, *Cultural Anthropology Online*, 8 May, 2013, http://culanth.org/fieldsights/213-the-ambivalence-ofmartyrs-and-the-counter-revolution

33   Al-Masry Al-Youm, "Usrat al-shahida Sally Zahran tanshur sura jadida laha bi-l-hijab 'ala Facebook" [Sally Zahran's family publish a new picture of her wearing the veil on Facebook], 20 February 2011.

34   Deniz Kandiyoti, "Disquiet and despair: The gender sub-texts of the 'Arab Spring,'" *Open Democracy*, 26 June 2012, http://www.opendemocracy.net/print/66458

35   Bill Ashcroft, *Post-Colonial Transformation* (London: Routledge, 2001), 47.

36   Bayat, *Life as Politics*, 98.

37   Roland Barthes, *Mythologies*, translated by Annette Lavers (New York: The Noonday Press, 1991), ed. 25, 115.

38   Judith Butler and Gayatri C. Spivak, *Who Sings the Nation-State?: Language, Politics, Belonging* (London: Seagull Books, 2007), 60.

39   Butler and Spivak, *Who Sings the Nation-State*, 61.

40   "Belly Dancer Safinaz Summoned for Insulting Egyptian Flag with Outfit," *Ahram Online*, 2014.

Notes to Chapter 3

1   Most women's narratives that deal with the Revolution or take it as a background of the plot are confined to 'narrating' what has happened. However, while it takes time to write novels that reflect on the Revolution, there are several testimonies and memoirs that are written in a subversive tone; for example, *Ismi thawra* (Revolution Is My Name) by Mona Prince is a strong memoir that exhibits a complete endorsement of the Revolution. (Arabic: *Ismi thawra*, Dar Merit, 2012; English translation: *Revolution Is My Name*, American University in Cairo Press, 2014).

2   Dana Gioia, "Can Poetry Matter?" *The Atlantic Monthly*, May 1991.

3   Edward Said, *Humanism and Democratic Criticism* (Palgrave Macmillan, 2004), 129.

4   Said, *Humanism and Democratic Criticism*, 28.

5   Theodor W. Adorno, "On Lyric Poetry and Society," *Notes to Literature* 1 (New York: Columbia University, 1991): 39.

6   Silence has been interpreted in many ways by feminists. For a survey of the various connotations of silence, see Carla Kaplan, "Women's Writings and Feminist Strategy," *American Literary History* 2, no. 2 (Summer 1990): 339–57. However, in the Arab culture, women are encouraged to adopt silence as a code of 'chastity.' That these young female poets decided to speak up and breach silence is a resistance strategy par excellence.

7   Teresa de Lauretis, *Alice Doesn't: Feminism, Semiotics, Cinema* (Bloomington: Indiana University Press, 1984), 2.

8   Liz Yorke, *Impertinent Voices: Subversive Strategies in Contemporary Women's Poetry* (London: Routledge, 1991), 15.

9   Sara Allam, *Doun athar li qobla* [Without a trace of a kiss] (Cairo: Dar Al Ain, 2013).

10   Sara Allam, *Tafuku azrar al-wehda* [Unbuttoning loneliness] (Cairo: Dar Al Ain, 2015).

11   Gilbert, Sandra, Introduction to *The Newly Born Woman*, translated by Betsy Wing (Manchester: Manchester University Press, 1986), 65.

12   Audre Lorde, *Sister Outsider: Essays and Speeches by Audre Lorde* (New York: The Crossing Press, 1984), 41.

13   Marwa Abu Daif, *Aqusu ayami wa anthuruha fi-l-hawa'* [I cut my days and scatter them in the air] (Cairo: Sharqiyat, 2013).

14   Mohamed Abu Zaid, "Marwa Abu Daif's 'I Cut My Days and Scatter Them in the Air': On the Aesthetics of Defeat and the Justification of Disappointment," *Al Quds Al Arabi*, 16 October 2013.

15   Adrienne Rich, *Of Woman Born: Motherhood as Experience and Institution* (London: Virago Books, 1977), 220.

16   Sabrin Mahran, *Targamat fi hiwariyat al-dama'ir* [Translations of consciences' dialogue] (Alexandria, Egypt: Dar Kalemh, 2014).

17   Interview with the poet in *al-Bedaya* electronic paper, 4 August 2014.

18   Liz Yorke, *Impertinent Voices*, 41.

19   Helen Cixous and Catherine Clement, "The Guilty One," *The Newly Born Woman*, 5.

20   Sara Abdeen, *'Ala hafatayn ma'an* [Together on two edges] (Cairo: Al Dar, 2014).

21   Luce Irigaray, *This Sex Which Is Not One*, translated by Catherine Porter and Carolyn Burke (New York: Cornell University Press, 1985), 30.

22   Liz Yorke, *Impertinent Voices*, 111.

23   Malak Badr, *Doun khasa'ir fadiha* [Without huge losses] (Cairo: Merit, 2011).

Notes to Chapter 4

1   Gilles Deleuze and Félix Guattari, *A Thousand Plateaus*, translated by Brian Massumi (Minneapolis: University of Minnesota Press, 1987), 7.

2   Deleuze and Guattari, *A Thousand Plateaus*, 8.

3   Michel Foucault, *Discipline and Punishment: The Birth of the Prison* (New York: Random House, 1975), 138.

4   Jurgen Habermas, "Modernity – An Incomplete Project," *The Anti-Aesthetic: Essays on Postmodern Culture*, edited by Hal Foster (New York: The New Press, 1998), 7.

5   Mikhail Bakhtin, *Problems of Dostoevsky's Poetics* (Minneapolis: University of Minnesota Press, 1993), 122–27.

6   Susan Stanford Friedman, *Mappings: Feminism and the Cultural Geographies of Encounter* (Princeton, NJ: Princeton University Press, 1998), 109.

7   Friedman is aware of all the theories that distinguish between space and place, where space signifies the preexisting entity that becomes a culturally constructed place. Yet, she believes that space is always "a form of cultural construction," *Mappings*, 261.

8   Friedman, *Mappings*, 109–110.

9   Suez was the first Egyptian city that had to stick to its guns in the face of incessantly thrown tear gas canisters, fired rubber bullets, and an enforced curfew in January 2011.

10 One of the scenes that attracted attention was the mingling on a friendly basis between Islamist men and non-veiled women; many have talked about it, and Caitlin Hawkins was an eyewitness: "A lasting image of that time for both my husband (Egyptian) and myself was of a young man with beard and gallabiya (so . . . probably member of MB or of similar persuasion) sitting on the kerb next to a young woman in jeans and t-shirt, both completely absorbed in their (to all appearances, non-confrontational) conversation."

11 Friedman, *Mappings*, 23.

12 Teresa de Lauretis, "Introduction," *Feminist Studies/Critical Studies*, edited by Teresa de Lauretis (Indiana University Press, 1986), 14.

13 Gayatri C. Spivak, "Can the Subaltern Speak?" *Marxism and the Interpretation of Culture*, edited by Cary Nelson and Lawrence Crossberg (Urbana: University of Illinois Press, 1988), 271–313.

14 Jacques Lacan, *Ecrits: A Selection (1966)*, translated by Alan Sheridan (New York: W.W. Norton & Co, 1977), 77.

15 Michael Rayan, "Identity Politics," in *The Encyclopedia of Literary and Cultural Theory*, Wiley-Blackwell, 2011 (online).

16 L.M. Alcoff, M. Hames-García, S. P. Mohanty, P.M.L. Moya, *Identity Politics Reconsidered* (New York: Palgrave Macmillan, 2006), 6.

17 In March 2011, a huge women's march celebrating International Women's Day turned ugly, and the participants were heckled and harassed. The next day, a few hundred protestors took to Tahrir Square again, and they were arrested. While men and women were tortured and jailed in the Egyptian Museum, and later in the military prison, women had to bear a bigger share of humiliation. In full view of several officers, they were forced to go through a series of virginity tests.

18 A personal experience. Ironically enough, I was on the street with other people celebrating the victory of Morsi when this happened.

19 Azza al-Garf was elected to the first parliament after 2011. Her views about women have often stirred a lot of controversies. Early in March 2012, she called for the cancellation of the antiharassment law, justifying her stance that by saying it is the indecent attire of women that invites harassment. Sawsan Gad, "We Mold the Collective Memory of Sexual Assault," *Egypt Independent*, 4 March 2012.

20 Patrick Kingsley, "Muslim Brotherhood Backlash against UN Declaration on Women's Rights," *The Guardian*, 15 March 2013.

21 Hoda Elsadda, "A War against Women: The CSW Declaration and the Muslim Brotherhood Riposte," *Open Democracy*, 3 April 2013, http://www.opendemocracy.net/5050/hoda-elsadda/war-against-women-csw-declaration-and-muslim-brotherhood-riposte

22 Bill Ashcroft, *Post-Colonial Transformation* (London: Routledge, 2001), 115.

23 Anne McClintock, "'No Longer in a Future Heaven': Gender, Race, and Nationalism," in *Dangerous Liaisons: Gender, Nation, and Postcolonial Perspectives*, edited by Anne McClintock, Aamir Mufti, and Ella Shohat (Minneapolis: University of Minnesota Press, 1997), 90.

24 Friedman, *Mappings*, 90.

25 Mona Eltahawy, "Why Do They Hate Us?" *Foreign Policy*, 23 April 2012, http://foreignpolicy.com/2012/04/23/why-do-they-hate-us/

26 Chandra Talpade Mohanty, *Feminism without Borders: Decolonizing Theory, Practicing Solidarity* (Duke University Press, 2003), 226.

27 "Tahrir Spirit" is a blog that compiled all reactions to Eltahawy's piece: http://tahrirspirit.blogspot.com/2012/04/compiled-list-of-eltahawy-reaction.html

28 "Mona: Why Do You Hate Us?" *Tahrir & Beyond*, 25 April 2013, http://theangryegyptian.wordpress.com/2012/04/25/mona-hate-us/

29 Deniz Kandiyoti, "Promise and peril: women and the 'Arab spring,'" *Open Democracy*, 8 March 2011, http://www.opendemocracy.net/print/58411

30 Deniz Kandiyoti, "Disquiet and despair: the gender sub-texts of the 'Arab Spring,'" *Open Democracy*, 26 June 2012 http://www.opendemocracy.net/print/66458

31 Kandiyoti, "Fear and fury: women and post-revolutionary violence," *Open Democracy*, 10 January 2013, https://www.opendemocracy.net/5050/deniz-kandiyoti/fear-and-fury-women-and-post-revolutionary-violence

32 Kandiyoti, "Promise and peril."

33 Kandiyoti, "Promise and peril."

34 Michel Foucault, *The History of Sexuality* 1 (New York: Random House, 1990), 95.

35 Teresa de Lauretis, "Feminist Studies/Critical Studies: Issues, Terms, and Contexts," *Feminist Studies/Critical Studies*, edited by Teresa de Lauretis (Indiana University Press, 1986), 8.

36 Asef Bayat, *Life as Politics: How Ordinary People Change the Middle East*, SIM Series on Contemporary Muslim Societies (Amsterdam: Amsterdam University Press, 2010), 97.

Notes to Chapter 5

1 The whole event is documented in *Without Reservation: The Beijing Tribunal on Accountability for Women's Human Rights*, edited by Niamh Reilly (Center for Women's Global Leadership, 1996).

2 Alifa Rif'at is the pen name of Fatima Abdullah Rif'at (1930–96). After her marriage, she gave in to the pressures of her husband to stop writing.

3 Marianne Hirsch and Valerie Smith, "'Feminism and Cultural Memory': An Introduction," *Signs: Journal of Women and Culture in Society* 28, no. 1 (Fall 2002): 4.

4 As much as they could, those researchers were trying to dismantle the 'add-women-and-stir method' approach, with the aim of curtailing the concept of "representation" making room for "re-presentation." See Gayatri C. Spivak, "Can the Subaltern Speak?" *Marxism and the Interpretation of Culture*, edited by C. Nelson and L. Crossberg (Urbana: University of Illinois Press, 1988), 271–313.

5 See website of Women and Memory: http://www.wmf.org.eg/en/about_ngo

6 See website of Women and Memory.

7 Pierre Nora, "Between Memory and History: Les Lieux de Memoire," *Theories of Memory: A Reader*, edited by Michael Rossington and Anne Whitehead (Baltimore: The Johns Hopkins University Press, 2007), 144–49.

8 Nora, "Between Memory and History," 149.

9 Maurice Halbwachs, *The Collective Memory (1950)*, translated by Francis J. Ditter, Jr. and Vida Yazdi Ditter (New York: Harper Colophon Books, 1980), 79.

10 *Al-Ahram Weekly*, 20 March, 2003.

11 Leila Ahmed, *Women and Gender in Islam: Historical Roots of a Modern Debate* (New Haven: Yale University Press, 1993).

12 Paul Connerton, *How Modernity Forgets* (New York: Cambridge University Press, 2009), 39.

13 Hirsch and Smith, "'Feminism and Cultural Memory,'" 4.

14 Halbwachs, *The Collective Memory*, 82.

15   Nora, "Between Memory and History, 146.

16   Doria Shafiq was a feminist, poet, editor, and one of the principle leaders of the women's movement in Egypt, starting from the mid-1940s.

17   "Heritage of Egypt's Women Will Not Be Undermined—NGOs," *Aswat Masriya*, 15 January 2013, http://en.aswatmasriya.com/news/view. aspx?id=95631838-9c4b-4a2c-b4c1-bc0571fc25e5

18   Walter Armbrust, "The Ambivalence of Martyrs and the Counter-Revolution," *Cultural Anthropology*, 8 May 2013, http://culanth.org/ fieldsights/213-the-ambivalence-of-martyrs-and-the-counter-revolution

19   Marwa Fikry Abdel Samei, "Taming Tahrir (Part One)," *Open Democracy*, 13 August 2013, http://www.opendemocracy.net/marwa-fikry-abdel-samei/ taming-tahrir-part-one

20   Jurgen Habermas, "Modernity: An Incomplete Project," *The Anti-aesthetic: Essays on Postmodern Culture*, edited by Hal Foster (New York: The New Press, 1998), 1–15.

21   Kevin Newmark, "Traumatic Poetry: Charles Baudelaire and the Shock of Laughter," *Explorations in Memory*, edited by Cathy Caruth (Baltimore: Johns Hopkins University Press, 1995), 238.

22   Dominick LaCapra, *History in Transit: Experience, Identity, Critical Theory* (Ithaca, NY: Cornell University Press, 2004), 112–17.

23   Available on YouTube: www.youtube.com/user/Leilzahra

24   Ghada Shahbender published a note on her Facebook page on 3 March 2014.

25   Hirsch and Smith, "'Feminism and Cultural Memory,'" 5.

26   "Tahrir Square Women's March Marred by Rival Protest," *The Guardian*, 8 March 2011.

27   Franz Fanon, *A Dying Colonialism* (New York: Grove Press, 1994).

28   Hoda Elsadda, "Egypt: The Battle over Hope and Morale," *Open Democracy*, 2 November 2011, http://www.opendemocracy.net/print/62390

29   Amnesty International: www.amnesty.org/en/news

30   Nicola Pratt, "Egyptian Women: Between Revolution, Counter-Revolution, Orientalism, and "Authenticity," *Jadaliyya*, 6 May 2013, http://www.jadali-yya.com/pages/index/11559/egyptian-women_between-revolution-counter

31   Deniz Kandiyoti, "Disquiet and despair: The gender sub-texts of the 'Arab Spring,'" *Open Democracy*, 26 June 2012, http://www.opendemocracy.net/ print/66458_

32   Sherine Seikaly, "The Meaning of Revolution: On Samira Ibrahim," *Jadaliyya*, 28 January 2013, http://www.jadaliyya.com/pages/index/9814/ the-meaning-of-revolution_on-samira-ibrahim#

33   In mid-December 2011, the woman who was stripped to her 'blue bra' and jeans by the police. In solidarity with her, the revolutionaries called her *sitt al-banat* (lady of the ladies) as a mark of honor. Her photograph was on the front page in all the local and in several of the international papers and magazines,

as a proof of the brutality of the regime, then the military junta. It is noteworthy here to mention that the infamous question, 'Why did she ever go there?' started with this incident in an attempt to condemn the girl. For a panoramic view of how the female body turned into a site of conflict, see, for example, Vickie Langohr, "'This Is Our Square': Fighting Sexual Assault at Cairo Protests," *MERIP* (Fall 2013), http://www.merip.org/mer/mer268/our-square

34 Hirsch and Smith, "'Feminism and Cultural Memory,'" 5.

35 Hirsch and Smith, "'Feminism and Cultural Memory,'" 6.

36 Hirsch and Smith, "'Feminism and Cultural Memory,'" 5.

37 W.J.T. Mitchell, "Image, Space, Revolution: The Arts of Occupation," *Critical Inquiry* 39, no. 1 (Autumn 2012): 8–32.

38 Homi Bhabha, *The Location of Culture* (London: Routledge, 1994), 89.

39 Ola Shahba gave her testimony in all available forms: broadcast on TV satellites, posted on YouTube, and circulated on the internet at http://www.nwrc.org

40 Maurice Halbwachs, *On Collective Memory*, translated and edited by Lewis Coser (Chicago: University of Chicago Press, 1992), 38.

41 Judith Butler, *Gender Trouble: Feminism and the Subversion of Identity* (London: Routledge, 1999), 173.

42 Fuada Watch and Op Anti-Sexual Harassment/Assault are the two major campaigns, among several others.

43 Paul Ricoeur, *Memory, History, Forgetting*, translated by Kathleen Blamey and David Pallauer (Chicago: Chicago University Press, 2004), 147.

44 LaCapra, *History in Transit*, 114.

45 Joan W. Scott, "Experience," *Feminists Theorize the Political*, edited by Judith Butler and Joan W. Scott (London: Routledge, 1992), 25.

46 Butler, *Gender Trouble*, 173.

47 In 2005, during a protest in solidarity with the judges in front of the Journalists Syndicate, a female journalist was sexually harassed by the thugs of the regime. The media (which is condemning the same acts now) vilified the woman, accusing her of lying, upon which her husband divorced her.

48 Chandra Talpade Mohanty, "Cartographies of Struggle: Third World Women and the Politics of Feminism," *Third World Women and the Politics of Feminism*, edited by Chandra Talpade Mohanty, Ann Russo, and Lourdes Torres (Bloomington, IN: Indiana University Press, 1991), 5.

49 Cathy Caruth, "Recapturing the Past: Introduction," *Trauma: Explorations in Memory* (Baltimore: Johns Hopkins University Press, 1995), 154.

50 LaCapra, *History in Transit*, 120.

51 Roland Barthes, *Camera Lucida: Reflections on Photography*, translated by Richard Howard (New York: Hill and Wang, 1981), 44.

52 Barthes, *Camera Lucida*, 96.

53 Marianne Hirsch and Leo Spitzer, "Testimonial Objects: Memory, Gender, and Transmission," *Poetics Today* 27, no. 2 (Summer 2006): 360.

54 *Popular Movements and Democratization in the Islamic World*, edited by Masatoshi Kisaichi (London: Routledge, 2006), 148.

55 Wulf Kansteiner, "Finding Meaning in Memory: A Methodological Critique of Memory Studies," *History and Theory* (May 2002): 184.

56 Asef Bayat, *Life as Politics: How Ordinary People Change the Middle East*, ISIM Series on Contemporary Muslim Societies (Amsterdam: Amsterdam University Press, 2010), 98.

57 Bayat, *Life as Politics*, 97.

58 Kansteiner, "Finding Meaning in Memory," 184.

59 Michael Rossington and Anne Whitehead, eds, "Introduction," *Theories of Memory: A Reader*, 11.

INDEX

Activism: academia 101; aesthetic 39;
    anti-occupation 30; art 39; feminism
    97, 101; online 57
Aesthetics: literary 39, 63, 69, 71; poli-
    tics 5, 7, 8, 35, 36, 37, 39, 42, 48, 71;
    women 38, 60, 62, 63, 69, 71
Agency 2, 39; female, within a national
    context 22, 23, 24, 25, 27, 91–94,
    98, 100; gender 31, 53, 86, 91; graf-
    fiti 43, 44, 49; geopolitical 32, 88,
    91–93, 98, 100, 112–13, 117, 127;
    literature 62, 65, 67; post-revolution
    19; post-structuralist 26, 31; wom-
    en's identity 2, 3, 4, 6, 7, 9, 24, 33
Art: politics 7, 8, 35, 36, 39, 40–43, 45,
    51, 53, 57, 117, 131; society 61, 85,
    114; street art 43–46, 48, 49, 121;
    women 10, 36, 38, 39, 53, 54, 109
Authoritarianism: elites 15, 19; Islamists
    93; military 73, 122, 123; regimes
    3, 15, 19, 131; women 93, 96, 97,
    103, 104

Binaries: gender 62, 74, 83; hierarchal
    75; political 27, 30, 36
Body: gender 8, 98, 124; literature 8, 63;
    politics 9, 10, 22, 52, 53, 55, 56, 85,
    87, 94, 95, 98, 102, 120, 125; viola-
    tions 9, 83, 86, 87, 91, 93, 96–98, 100,
    119, 120, 124–27; women 4, 5, 8, 9,

46, 47, 52, 53, 55, 56, 85, 86, 87, 91,
    94–98, 100, 119, 120, 122, 124–27

Citizenship 9, 55, 56, 85, 114; gender
    47, 56; graffiti 48, 49, 52; media 57,
    87; political 114; women 19, 22, 37,
    38, 87, 98

Dialectics: cultural memory 118, 131;
    gender 121; identity 26, 67, 74; liter-
    ature 67, 74; political 28, 38, 48, 66;
    women 123
Discourse 2, 6, 25, 28, 48, 57, 121,
    126, 131; 25 January Revolution 6,
    61; dominant 31, 36, 54, 109, 113;
    feminist 4, 7, 14, 15, 18, 20, 26, 27,
    33, 38, 40, 52, 53, 55, 57, 62, 68, 69,
    93–96, 104, 105; gender 3, 8, 10,
    22, 32, 33, 35, 36, 38, 59, 60, 97, 98,
    122, 125; hegemonic 121; identity
    26–29, 39, 92, 97; Islamist 27, 28,
    53, 54, 93, 97, 105, 130; literature
    62, 68, 69, 73, 78, 81, 82; national 3,
    38, 103; sociopolitical 11, 30, 36–38,
    40, 51, 52, 82, 87, 90–92, 96, 120;
    street art 49
Diversity 3, 19, 37, 113, 114; art 42;
    ethnic 21; inclusion of women 15,
    23, 87, 110; religious 21; sociopolit-
    ical 22

Experience: 25 January Revolution 11,
42, 70, 87, 114–16; agency 25, 94;
culture 29; democracy 87; gender 9,
122; identity 93, 94; literature 79,
80, 82; street art 49; violence 98,
124–26; women 11, 23, 33, 79, 80,
82, 93–95, 98, 104, 116

Feminism 4, 14, 18, 28, 32, 47, 92, 128;
cultural 7; discourse 4; FEMEN
52; global 18, 32; gender activists
14, 30, 32, 112; geopolitical 88,
99, 100; harassment 94; Islam 21;
language and silence 62; literature
68, 72, 109; National Council for
Women 92; nationalism 4, 7, 19–21,
23; political 18, 27, 32; post-revolutionary 8, 14, 18, 26, 27, 29, 31,
32, 46, 59, 101, 103, 104; Shaarawi,
Huda 112; state 16, 104, 110, 111,
113; street art 45, 47; television 50;
western 7, 25, 109

Gender 31, agency 2, 5, 22; Algerian
revolution 7; art and street art 7,
35, 36, 41, 44, 45, 60, 62; cultural
memory 128; feminism 7; constructs and roles 18, 23, 27, 35, 36,
47, 52, 57, 60, 63, 74, 86, 91, 124;
geopolitical 88, 89, 97, 102, 119;
identity 2, 4, 5, 6, 7, 8, 16, 26, 28,
32, 33, 38, 47, 59, 89, 110, 121,
124, 126; intersectionality 14, 26,
28, 32, 88, 100, 125; movements
and protests 13, 14, 15, 47, 109,
122, 124; nationalism 3, 4, 6, 7, 19,
23, 38, 47, 52, 53; oppression and
marginalization 1–4, 9, 14, 16, 22,
23, 41, 53, 90, 93, 98, 100; political
10, 97, 102, 112, 125; revolutionary
and post-revolutionary discourse
3–8, 11, 23, 33, 37, 38, 44, 48, 49,
59, 86, 87, 91, 92, 109, 116, 119;
social media 57; western violence
9, 23, 98, 100, 124, 126; women's
issues and rights 1–5, 8, 10, 23, 26,
46, 49, 52, 85, 110, 119
Graffiti: artists 44, 45, 46, 49, 121;
gender 52; iconic 43, 45; literature
43, 49; Mohamed Mahmoud 43;

nationalism 46; resistance 8, 10,
42–45, 48, 49, 53, 123, 130; social
media 44; violence 43, 44, 45, 47;
visual 42, 52; women 36, 43, 44, 45,
46, 47, 52, 53, 121

Herstory 20, 70, 108, 110, 112, 116
History 3, 10, 31, 111; activists 54;
gender 3, 104, 109, 118; graffiti 43,
48; literature 60, 63, 72; local 48;
martyrs 51; memory 110, 111, 113,
116, 118; nationalism 3, 11; sociopolitical 37, 89, 113, 118; social media
116; Tahrir and 25 January 89, 118;
women 3, 11, 20, 21, 51, 54, 63, 68,
72, 101, 104, 109, 110, 111

Iconic women 52, 54, 55, 79, 110, 120,
122
Identity 4, 6, 23, 24, 26, 27, 29, 30, 32,
37, 44, 47, 48, 90, 111, 113, 114,
121, 122, 130; 25 January Revolution 2, 51, 91; agency 44; collective
115; culture 23, 88, 92, 98, 110;
discourse 2, 26, 29, 97; Egyptian
2; experience 25; feminist 28, 94;
gender 2, 4, 5, 6, 7, 16, 33, 47, 89,
121, 122, 126; global 26; Islamic
98; literature 8, 65, 68; local 26, 41,
89; male 65; memory 10; politics
5, 21, 85, 86, 96, 113; religion 51;
post-structuralist 25; women 9, 21,
23, 28, 38, 46, 51, 53, 65, 68, 81, 93,
98, 122
Islamism: activists and movements 123;
discourses of the state 20; graffiti
43, 45; presidency 27; revolutionary
scene 6; women 27, 28, 53, 56, 88,
93, 94, 95, 96, 97, 102, 124; rise to
power and regime 53, 60, 92, 93, 97,
98, 101; violence against women 95,
96, 102, 124

Law: family 22; lawsuits 45, 50, 52, 119,
121; of the father 73, 76, 77, 81, 83;
of non-governmental organizations
92; personal status 16, 17, 22; post-
25 January Revolution 56; protest
law 40; women's rights 16, 17, 20,
21, 22, 45, 52, 100

Margins: gender 48; identity 36, 48;
    literature 59, 78, 79; power 41, 42,
    108; women 38, 54, 59, 109–144
Memory: 25 January Revolution 114–16,
    117; collective 112–13, 122; cultural
    10, gender 5, 119, 122; history 111,
    116, 128–32; identity 111, 114; liter-
    ature 66, 67, 68; politics 5, 107, 108,
    110, 113, 119, 120, 122, 127; power
    107; resistance 8, 108; 112, 118;
    social media 116–117; street art 121;
    trauma 67, 76, 114, 123–27; visual
    131; women 10, 55, 107, 109–110,
    113, 119, 120, 122, 123–26
Micropolitics: gender 47; identity 5, 47;
    nationalism 47; women 5, 6, 23, 50,
    130
Military 29; arrests 24, 44, 96, 99, 119;
    graffiti 43–44, 121; literature 69, 72,
    73; memory 124; nationalism 23;
    ousting of Morsi 30; resistance 60,
    120, 121; violations 2, 44, 45, 51–52,
    94, 96, 99, 120; violence 102; women
    2, 24, 45, 51–52, 54, 94, 96, 102,
    119, 120, 122
Multiplicity 18, 42, 86, 113

Narratives: 25 January Revolution 5, 11,
    24, 32, 59; gender 5, 11, 32; graffiti
    48; history 68; literature 59; memory
    125, 127; patriarchal 10; sacred 76;
    Tahrir Square 91; women 24, 59
Nationalism: 25 January Revolution 6;
    cultural 38; Egyptian 3, 11, 55–57;
    feminist 4, 7, 19, 20, 21, 23; gender
    3, 4, 6, 19–23, 47, 52, 56; Islamist
    22; military 23; patriarchal 4; post-
    colonial 4; rise of 3; women 46,
    55–57, 103, 110

Patriarchy: gender 74; internal misog-
    yny/false consciousness 9; literature
    62, 73; misogyny 5, 102; patriarchal
    narrative 10, 82, 86, 87; patriarchal
    state 38, 54, 76, 77, 81, 101, 102, 103
Polarization: gender 9, 23; identity 23,
    political 98; women 23, 51, 86, 98
Position: discourse 7, 25, 32, 93, 126;
    ethical 53; gender 4, 10, 11, 48, 88,
    91, 125; geography 26, 27; graffiti

45; humanist 61; identity 24, 26, 28,
    29, 90; legal 17; literature 68, 69, 70,
    73, 75, 77, 78, 79, 81, 82; martyr-
    dom 51; memory 10, 107; new art
    36; new text 41, 47, 48, 51; political
    8, 25, 30, 36; popular 40; post-25
    January Revolution 4, 42; power
    relations 41, 42; subjectivity 37;
    women 6, 7, 8, 10, 15, 17, 18, 19, 22,
    26, 27, 36, 38, 46, 47, 51, 56, 85, 93,
    94, 96, 98, 100, 101, 104, 108, 124;
    women's agency 24–25; women's
    rights 18, 22, 92, 103
Power: 25 January Revolution 71, 96;
    authoritarian 10, 73, 93, 95, 96, 97,
    103, 120, 122; boycott 25; distribu-
    tion 10; external 38; gender 44, 48,
    91, 98, 126; Islamist 93, 123; litera-
    ture 66, 70, 74, 75, 76; memory 113,
    114, 117, 118, 122; new text 40, 41,
    42, 57; art 42, 43, 53; of presence 8,
    42, 47, 54, 87, 104, 130; of the central
    state 3, 110; of the patriarch 2, 65,
    87, 94; oppression 23, 26, 28, 94,
    107, 108; relations 3, 4, 7, 9, 10, 23,
    39, 40, 41, 42, 59, 68, 78, 85, 86, 91,
    92, 93, 98, 101, 102, 103, 107, 109,
    112; psychological 64; sociopolitical
    64, 68, 78, 111, 113; women's agency
    6, 31, 53, 93, 95, 97, 100, 108, 124;
    women's rights 22
Presence: literature 75, 77; memory 123;
    patriarchy 77; politics of absence
    74, 75, 123; power of 8, 42, 47, 54,
    130; representation 49; women 4,
    5, 14, 15, 24, 27, 36, 53, 56, 86, 87,
    88, 92, 93, 95, 97, 98, 104, 114, 118,
    123, 130

Rhizome 85, 86
Representation: cultural 16, 23, 41, 98,
    120; memory 121, 122, 128; of the
    Other 18; street art 49; women 39,
    82, 93, 95
Resistance 3, 6, 8, 32, 42, 54, 62, 64, 85,
    89, 95, 103, 104, 120, 129; artistic
    expression 7, 35, 44, 45, 121; litera-
    ture 72, 82, 125; memory 108, 113,
    130; women 5, 9, 31, 32, 44, 52, 97,
    120, 123

Revolution: acts 3, 36, 44, 47, 104, 131; consciousness 104; context 27, 31, 47; discourse 25, 38, 91, 92, 93, 97, 120; gender 47; generation 5, 7, 9, 86; graffiti 43, 44, 48, 49; imagination 87; language 41; literature 11; paraphernalia 50; post-25 January Revolution 101, 129; protestors 99; scene 6; socialist party 14, 100; spirit 86

Self 24, 28, 48, 67, 82, 89, 126; gender 60, 65, 66, 68, 94; literature and language 70, 76, 78, 80, 81; self-consciousness 104; self-development 11; self-knowledge 83; self-worth 66; and other 48
Silence: graffiti 45, 46; knowledge 82; literature 72, 75, 76, 79; memory 123; resistance 62, 66, 67, 108, 119, 120, 126, 127; suppression 3, 30, 31, 45, 46, 62, 97, 119, 120, 125
Space: alternative 43; for women 10, 11, 23, 38; of appearance 3, 4; private 89, 90; public 42, 43, 47, 48, 51, 54;
Subject: binary oppositions 75; gender 4, 48, 53, 87, 91; of feminist writing 68, 69; positions 8, 24, 25, 27, 28, 90, 93, 126; subject matter 44, 66; women 3
Subjectivity: collective 40, 88, 89, 91; consciousness 104, 127; female 86, 91, 93; identity 37; in literature 77, 80, 81, 83; post-structuralist 28; women's agency 27, 67

Subversion 3, 9, 59, 62, 73, 78, 82, 123

Tahrir Square 3, 13, 14, 21, 24, 28, 50, 87, 88, 89, 91, 95, 114, 119, 123, 124
Testimony 30; against violence 99, 124, 125; trauma 127
Text: gender 8; iconic 54; the female body 4, 5; new aesthetic text 36, 39, 42; new national 57; new text 7, 8, 35, 37, 40, 41, 45, 47, 48, 57, 121; oppositional 5; revolutionary 5, 8, 31; visual 42, 44, 47, 48, 50, 51, 54
Tradition 6; art 41, 52, 90; bourgeois culture 41, 48; consciousness 37; gender 52, 65, 68, 78; hierarchy 40; home 89; literary 27; social 68; traditionalism 103
Trauma: 25 January Revolution 114, 115; abuse 120, 124, 125; gender 122; graffiti 121; historical 116; memory 67, 118, 126; narration 125, 127; post-traumatic 78, 125; structural 116

Victims 125, abuse 2; gender 124; literature 82; victimization 28
Voice: activist 19; feminist 18; graffiti 47; memory 107, 124; outsider 31; poetry 8, 59, 60, 61, 63, 78, 79, 83; protesting 14; resistance 62, 119; rising generation 6, 11, 23, 33; suppression 97, 108; women 8, 10, 23, 46, 53, 60